The Lion, the Dung Beetle and the Veld Tool Box

20 Bush Tales from Southern Africa

The Lion, the Dung Beetle and the Veld Tool Box

20 Bush Tales from Southern Africa

David Bristow

First published by Jacana Media (Pty) Ltd in 2021

10 Orange Street
Sunnyside
Auckland Park 2092
South Africa
+2711 628 3200
www.jacana.co.za

© David Bristow, 2021

All rights reserved.

ISBN 978-1-4314-3190-8

Also available as an ebook.

Cover design by publicide
Editing by Megan Mance
Proofreading by Lara Jacob
Set in Minion Pro 10.8/15PT
Printed by Shumani
Job no. 003849

See a complete list of Jacana titles at www.jacana.co.za

*This book is dedicated
to the memory of*

*Belhauser (Bell)
the cutest little bush critter I ever knew*

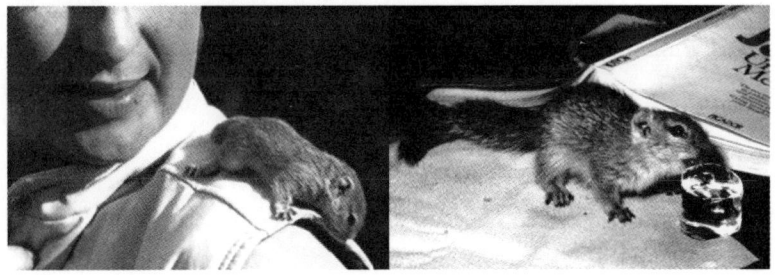

Contents

Introduction 1

1. Lions and Lion Men: Imagine Africa Without Them 3
2. Leaping Lizards, Predatory Giraffes and Other Game Ranger Myths and Legends 15
3. Of ~~Mice~~ Gerbils and ~~Men~~ Boys: Three Lads Go on a Very Big Adventure 23
4. Antelope and Evolution: When Whales Walked, Giraffes had Short Necks and WTF is a Gerenuk Anyway? 35
5. Goggas and the Veld Tool Box 43
6. Elephants: Pachyderm Proceedings with Some Very Bulky Parts .. 55
7. One Loony Bird, a Funny Monkey and the Most Barefaced Botanical Heist in History 67
8. "We're Okay, We have Fire": Five Go on an Even Bigger Adventure 79
9. Why the Long Neck? Giraffes and the Long and the Short of Adaptive Biology 89
10. A Most Propitious Paddle: The Saga of a Hippo, a Crocodile, a Buffalo and Some Very Fortunate Humans 99
11. Women in the Wilderness: Sisters are Doing It for Themselves 107

12. Animal Intelligence: Stand Back, We're Not Sure How Deep This Thing Goes 123

13. The Octopus, a Wiggly Worm and Us 133

14. Seldom Seen at the Place of New Beginnings 139

15. An Inordinate Fondness for Tortoises 151

16. Big Bertie's Broken Heart 157

17. The Honeyguide Effect: A Mnemonic for Our Home in the Wilderness 163

18. Ladies and Gentlemen, We Present, the Beetles and the Rolling Dungballs! 173

19. Camp Life and Pets: They're Family But It Seldom Ends Well 181

20. The Hunters, the Hunted and the Balance of Nature 195

Introduction

WHEN I FIRST HIT ON the idea of writing these "stories from the veld", this one of safari tales and bush legends was the one I actually had in mind. But, as my good old mate John Lennon once put it, life happened in between.

My original idea was to collect and collate the many stories I'd heard over the years from safari guides, hunters and people around a hundred campfires in Africa. However, when I started trying to prise them out of people they all clammed up. At first I thought it might be stage fright, or performance anxiety at the sight of pen and paper or pocket recorder. I later deduced that each of them were amassing their own compendiums of stories for the bestseller they were going write – one day.

So I collected my own and here are the best of them. One thing that has befallen me over the intervening years (given that the first incident related here took place around 40 years ago) is that my memory might not be the honed rapier of intellect it once was. But then again, as my other good mate Donald said when I asked him about one incident in which he was involved: don't worry too much about the facts getting in the way of a good story.

These tales are as true to history as can be ascertained, or as memory allows. Excepting when they aren't. Either way, when the spirit in the glass releases the genie of the wild, there's an element of truth under every bush legend. Call me a mythomaniac if you will, I put it down to my admiration for the old bushveld raconteur Schalk Lourens.

Lions and Lion Men: Imagine Africa Without Them

HAVE YOU NOTICED HOW NUMEROUS "lion men" over the years all started looking like their subjects. Think of the doyen of them all, George Adamson (when we got to know him in older age), with his deeply tanned and prune-like skin, long grey locks and substantial grizzled beard; Zimbabwean safari guide Steve Pope (also deceased); Botswana-based wildlife filmmaker Dereck Joubert; or lion researcher and general lion fundi Chris McBride, last seen running amok in Kafue National Park in Zambia. If you could line them up, each at the same age, adding a lion or two, you'd be hard pressed to tell them apart in a suspect line-up.

Of them I know (or knew) Steve Pope the best, and I went on numerous walking safaris with him in Mana Pools National Park. He only played his ace card in select company: if you knew your dog from your cat spoor, and you went in October – the hot, dry, dusty suicide month in the Zambezi Valley – with luck he'd take you to Chitake Spring. At that time of year the one-kilometre spring line becomes a killing zone for two lion dynasties that have ruled their respective ends for many generations. Steve would think little of walking among them, even when (as I well recall) they were busy on a buffalo kill, or pulling the tail of a sleeping cat.

Most clearly I remember the time when, walking with Steve and some mates, he in his trademark sweat-stained leather hat, he shouldered his rifle in preparation for deflecting a charging lion. "Oh drat," he said, or something like that. "I forgot the bullets."

Not easily intimidated, he told us to hold our ground and our focus till the last moment when, he reckoned, given our superior numbers, the lion would come to a skidding halt a few metres from us. That was when we should drop our gaze so as not to challenge the king, and back off smoothly but as swiftly as we could without making it look like we were in a rush. I never did figure out if he was in complete control, or just bungled his way through these things.

The thing with Steve was that he thought he was a lion. In a way he was, but not in the way most of us would understand. Some time before I met him, Steve had been inducted into their tribe by the Kavinga people of the Zambezi escarpment where he operated. Theirs was the lion totem and in Steve they saw the reincarnation of their own kindred spirit. Each trip with him was guaranteed to be a big adventure. It wasn't a big cat that took him in the end, though, but the other Big C, in 2011.

Uncle Ossie was another. Family holidays to Zimbabwe and a relative's ranch near Great Zimbabwe, where my brothers and I would get to ride on zebras, run around after warthogs, stroke cheetahs and pet lions, persist in my mythology of astonishing things. The patriarch housed, habituated and trained orphaned wild animals and made a living hiring them out for movies. Back in the 1960s and '70s, whenever you saw a supposedly wild African animal "attacking" someone, odds were it was one of Uncle Ossie's.

His favourite was Dandelion, or Dandy for short, really more like the family dog than a king of the jungle. Dandy had been found down an aardvark hole in the Hwange area after a veld fire had ravaged the place. The cub was not yet fully weaned and its mother must have stuffed it down the hole when she saw the raging fire approaching. She was nowhere to be seen so Ossie took the weeny thing home and hand reared it.

One day Dandy was starring in a film shoot based at Lanseria Airport when it was still just an airstrip in the peri-urban belt of outer Johannesburg. He was supposed to have been secured inside a tennis court for the night, but somehow was not, or he managed to break out of what to him would have been no more constraining than the proverbial paper bag.

One of the cameramen, who had decided to sleep outside on a

stretcher, was awakened by hot breath puffing on his face. It was Dandy looking for someone to play with. The man screamed and starting trying to fend off the huge predator. Dandy did what any self-respecting lion would and chomped down on the poor man's head, killing him almost instantly. Ossie knew it meant the end of his furred companion, and Dandelion was duly dispatched.

When the Mugabe regime expropriated their farm Le Rhone, the operation moved closer to Harare. One morning there, Ossie's son Viv discovered the remains of a man inside a lion enclosure at their Lion and Cheetah Park. The park had 32 lions, but four "very bad ones" were kept in their own smaller run, Viv explained to the media. It seemed the man, probably starving, saw some chunks of meat over a fence and decided to chance it, but he chose a very high-risk fence to jump.

Renowned lion researcher George Schaller noted that the life of a male lion in Africa, specifically the Serengeti, is short and brutal. As soon as it loses its physical prowess an alpha male will be set upon by the next contender to the crown in line. The reigning king might win the first few battles, but by age six or tops seven, a younger, stronger male will overpower him and either kill him or drive him out of pride and territory.

The end of Ossie the lion man of Great Zimbabwe came not in the ivory teeth of another lion but the iron jaws of what the French call a chemin de fer. It happened at a lonely level railway crossing, but as to why it happened no one else knew. One particular horse of iron proved to be his last, but by then the old bush man had lived longer and fuller than most.

The most eccentric of them all though was, and still is as far as I know, Chris McBride (author of *The White Lions of Timbavati*). Even in a place like Maun, where he holed up for some years to conduct lion research, a place that attracts more offbeats than a Jack Kerouac requiem, Chris was considered a bit odd. The competition was stiff, what with the likes of Barefoot Pete, Oddball Lance and Monkey-Eater Ian.

Their saloon of choice was the fabled Duck Inn, ruled firmly by Bernadette, Mma Duck, small in stature but only fools underestimated her leadwood temperament. And if that did not deter the most incautious of patrons, her partner, a herculean, blond-haired Scandinavian named Soren, would sort you out.

Soren was a PH, or professional hunter, the highest rank in the community and type specimen for Thor. By comparison he would make Chris Hemsworth, even when suited up for the role, look like a boy on his first day at school. I'm not sure whether or not Soren was there on the day in question, but most of the regulars were. Most of the regulars usually were, unless they were out hunting one thing or another.

A visiting American journalist around 1990 described the place not as an inn but a bar, abutting the airport of this booming Kalahari sandveld town of 20 000, "about 200 of them non-black". It was frequented by bush pilots, hunters, itinerant journalists, various business types, mysterious women, government officials and safari goers. If Humphrey Bogart, Claude Rains, Peter Lorre and Sidney Greenstreet shared the same table, wrote one David B. Wilson, they would fit right in.

It was a slow summer's day at the Duck Inn some time back in 19-voetsek. The place was hellishly hot and close (what the safari companies had recently begun trying to sell as the "green season") and the patrons were bored. Flies buzzed annoyingly, neglected beers spoiled if not duly attended. The solid tabletops, selected for durability more than looks, bore the scars of many a debate of whose hunting knife had the superior blade.

It was into this lions' den that what we must presume was a nice young couple (but we'll never know for sure) with matching safari outfits ventured, hoping for some coolth and comfort in which to wait for an onward flight. You could have cut the atmosphere with a Leatherman.

All the lions and even lionesses looked up. Had they been more experienced, the interloping couple might have sensed danger and run for it, but they did not. This was Africa and they had paid big bucks for an adventure. No one remembers who started the fray, or why, but when old-timers of Maun reflect on the incident the name of Barefoot Pete usually pops up.

Each table at the Duck Inn had a condiment set of salt and pepper and two of those plastic squeegee bottles, one red for tomato sauce and the other for the mustard. It could have been the heat, or the beer, but one of the patrons sitting behind the safari couple picked up the squeegee bottles from his table and drew parallel stripes, one red and the other mustard, down one of the poor unfortunates' steam-pressed khaki jackets.

Someone else joined and did the same to the other. In no time radio-active streams of red and yellow were flying through the air and plastering the traumatised couple in gloopy, gharish condiment. Fighting through arcing streams of noxious food additive, they fled the place in cries and tears. It was a safari they would never forget.

Maun was like that back then.

Thinking back on it, Soren was most likely off on some hunting lark. Seeing his torso without a covering shirt was like looking at the trunk of an African teak tree that has been used as a lion's scratching post. Heavy scars ran down his mahogany-tanned, muscular arms, neck and back. They were all thanks to an American woman named Sissy and her son who had come out to Africa to kill a lion as a kind of coming-into-manhood right of passage.

In order to blood them, the clients were taken first into the Kalahari to do some gamebird shooting, followed by two days in the Okavango shooting things like zebra. Having acclimatised to the dense acacia bush and general lie of the land, they went off in search of the lion whose number rang up when the licence to shoot it had been purchased – $35 000, *ka-ching*!

Trackers Joseph and Teko spotted a lioness and cubs, and watched as they ran off into the cover of dense candle-thorn bushes, a tough, spiky shrub also known as *duma tau* (where the lion sleeps). Soren steered the open-sided 4x4 through the dense growth and noted a large dark-maned male slink off into the shade of some mopane trees close by. The pro hunter got his client into a good shooting position, but the young man was shaking so badly when he did eventually get off a shot (and here I feel it pertinent to note that the distance was good for hitting a tin beer can with an air rifle), it scored only a flesh wound at which the lion bolted back into dense cover.

Back in the Land Rover, Soren steered towards the duma tau, when out from the tangle the enraged cat broke cover and leaped right onto the back of the vehicle. The driver floored the Landy, throwing it repeatedly hard to left and then right. This managed to dislodge the fearsome claws from the tailgate and the lion slunk back into cover.

Doing what any good hunter must, the PH needed to go back and make good the shoot. He asked the clients if they were game, but they were clearly in no state to walk, let alone shoot, straight. Sandgrouse and zebra were one thing, but grovelling around in dust in the hope of dispatching an angry lion was more than they'd paid for. So, Soren put the American woman into a large leadwood tree, and he and the trackers went off to follow the tracks, with the young would-be trophy hunter well in the rear.

Of all the things you might fear, being ambushed by a 250-kilogram concentration of muscle, sinew, teeth and talons that is a male African lion should be right near top of your list. It will grab you with most of its 18 claws; four on each paw plus a dewclaw on each of the front ones. Those weapons of mass destruction are usually around four centimetres long, hard as carbon steel and sharp as razors. They can do a large amount of harm to a soft-skinned body.

Then come the fangs, specifically the canines that are the killing teeth. They grow to around 10 centimetres and can tear into even buffalo and elephant hide, or sever the spine of a hippo. Although the bite force of a lion is nowhere near that of, say, a spotted hyena (1 100-psi), or a Nile crocodile (3 500-psi), the 650-pounds-per-square-inch chomp of a fully mature lion, when it bears down on just four points each the size and shape of a steak-knife tip, can quite easily cut clean through a human arm, even one that looks like a teak branch.

A male lion's roar is something quite extraordinary in the animal world. A defining feature of the big cats is that they do roar, unlike others which only grunt, hiss or purr. When it does roar in earnest the very ground seems to vibrate and, if you are close, you will shake with raw emotion. The reason is in its larynx, or voice box.

If you strip off its skin a lion's body looks very much like a honed human bodybuilder. Excepting that it has a very much bigger larynx. The strap muscles that pull it backwards when vocalising, unlike ours which are connected in our necks, are anchored way down in its ribcage to ribs two and three. They act like the slide of a trombone, pulling it far back so that the instrument is very much bigger than ours, and also much longer. Also, its mouth opens into a much bigger tuba shape than our puny clarinets.

The roar of a lion marking its territory can be heard up to eight or nine kilometres distant. It leaves no one in doubt as to who's the boss. Lions have at least nine distinct vocalisation meanings, from come and join me (to a coalition partner), through back off, to come and try me and, I'm coming for *you*! That's one you don't want to hear when walking in the bush.

Soren was walking with his .458, looking for spoor, when the lion roared and charged. It happened so suddenly the shot Soren fired instinctively missed. The lion floored him and bit down into his right shoulder. Down on the ground, the giant Swede knew his best chance of survival was to play dead, but to cover his neck with one arm in order to protect his spine. During the tussle Joseph grabbed the lion's tail and was trying to pull it off the prone man, when it turned on him.

The enraged lion repeatedly bit into Joseph's right arm. Meanwhile Teko had treed himself, while the American lad had jumped into the Land Rover's driving seat. First, he drove under the tree where Teko clung so the tracker could drop down into the vehicle. Then he manoeuvred it between the lion and its quarry, Joseph. Teko and the lad managed to lift Joseph into the vehicle but then, instead of trying to fetch Soren, or shoot the lion, as the trackers were now yelling for him to do, the boy drove to the tree where his mother was enjoying a grand-stand view, so that she could jump down and get into the vehicle. At this stage the two clients broke down into a sobbing, heaving huddle (according to Teko).

Finally, they did drive to where Soren was lying and managed to get him aboard, with blood flowing copiously. Attempts were made to staunch the flow of blood from both injured men, while Teko managed to radio HQ in Maun. A hunter named Tim was dispatched to retrieve them, which he did about two hours later. Joseph Humpty and Soren Dumpty spent two and three-and-a-half months, respectively, in hospital being put back together again.

It was finally the legendary hunter Harry Selby (made famous in the writings of Robert Ruark while he, Selby, was a young hunter working in Kenya),[1] who took on the task of locating and delivering the coup de grace to the ill-fated sovereign of the bush. At least it was one lion that never left African shores with its head mounted on a wooden shield, but was assigned a warrior's end, lying where it fell to be deconstructed by the litany of creatures assigned garbage detail: vultures and hyenas, jackals and crows, beetles, flies and their maggots, bacteria and finally funguses. Unto dust.

WHILE THE WORLD'S CONSERVATION ATTENTION is focused largely on rhino, elephant and pangolin poaching, the big cats of Africa are not faring much better. Cheetahs are down to a pitiful number from their historical range across Africa, Europe and Asia. Their numbers have dropped 90 per cent over the past 100 years with the majority of the estimated 7 000 or fewer survivors living in Southern Africa. Cheetah DNA diversity is extremely compromised, with every living individual today being the equivalent of a brother, sister or cousin, which of course speaks poorly of their chances for long-term survival.

Leopards in Africa are far more plentiful than both lions and cheetahs, but they too come under extreme hunting pressure from stock farmers, poachers as well as trophy hunters. In South Africa leopard skins and teeth are highly prized cultural symbols, so a good amount of the spoils pass through the muti trade of traditional healers. Go to any muti shop in the country and you can bet on finding a leopard skin there. As human populations expand and become increasingly affluent, so the demand for animal "parts" increases, while wildlife numbers tumble in freefall.

Even in the so-called legal hunting business, the pressure is

---

[1] Harry Selby was born in the Free State, but his family moved to Kenya when he was a youngster. Leaving the family farm, he found a job as a mechanic for the hunting company Ker & Downey, where Philip Percival mentored him. Percival himself had acquired worldwide fame leading safaris for the likes of Teddy Roosevelt, Ernest Hemingway and Baron Rothschild. By 1977, when sports hunting was banned in Kenya, Ker & Downey relocated to Botswana. From there Selby led the operation until he retired in 2000. He died in Maun in 2018 at age 92.

on. Every hunter wants to bag a lion. Together with the "Rowland Ward" syndrome (after the publication that lists trophy records), they all want a big alpha male nailed to some parlour wall or stuffed in some garish attack pose for a mansion's entrance foyer. But with decreasing numbers of big trophy-size males, professional hunters must use all their wiles to come up with a suitable animal and its hefty price tag. Every hunter is looking for an ever-diminishing Rowland Ward listing.

Remember the lion named Cecil? He was a seriously big alpha male, one that could well have earned the person who killed him an entry in Rowland Ward. Cecil was the subject of a long-ongoing research project in Zimbabwe's Hwange National Park, and wore a clearly visible neck transmitter collar to show for it. While many people around the world vilified the hunter, American dentist Walter Palmer, for the lion's death, that man was only partly to blame.

The person most responsible for this highly irresponsible and unethical killing was his pro hunter, Theo Bronkhorst. He would have known Cecil as one of two alpha males in the area all too well, a lion that had lived there for an amazing 13 years (in large part due to the absence of any competition due to decreasing numbers there). With the telescopic sights affixed to modern hunting rifles, there is no ways, none in hell, a PH as well as his client would not see a large animal sporting a GPS collar.

Equally heinous was the fact that Palmer, a bow hunter, only wounded Cecil with an arrow. The lion was dispatched only the following day with a death shot. Then they (we can assume it was the professional hunter, or on his orders) buried the collar. However, more the fools they, it carried right on bleeping and led researchers from Oxford University's Wildlife Conservation Research Unit right to it. For his efforts, Bronkhorst's operation pocketed a cool US $45 000. A Zimbabwean court cleared him on a charge of illegal hunting: he had a permit to shoot a lion, he shot a lion. There are no sovereign laws protecting collared lions, only universal ethics.

AT ONE TIME LIONS WERE considered to be the most successful land mammals on Earth – after humans. The scientific name for lion,

Panthera leo, comes from ancient Greek *pan* (all), *ther* (predator) and *leon* (lion). However, they are now listed as "vulnerable" on the International Union for the Conservation of Nature's Red List. To put actual figures to this, 50 years ago there were an estimated 100 000 lions in Africa. Today there are only around 25 000: a decline of 75 per cent.

That is fewer than the number of cyclists who set off each year on the Cape Town Cycle Tour: a truly shocking statistic – especially so given that it has happened in many of our lifetimes. By contrast, the human population has – there is no better word – exploded. This has in turn created the need for additional land to grow crops, run livestock and expand settlements. No peasant farmer or pastoralist would choose a lion as his or her neighbour.

As human communities and protected areas compete for space, conflict between people and predators becomes inevitable. The loss of habitat and natural prey animals are the main causes of lion deaths across Africa. The rolling effect of this is that it leads to predation of stock and then revenge killings for the loss of livestock. Communities and farmers bordering on national parks have become increasingly intolerant of marauding predators, due in large part to their seeing park authorities as being friends of wildlife, to their detriment.

It's true that a number of conservation and safari companies has implemented stock-loss compensation schemes, but they have proved to be only partly curative (when they are not abused by wily farmers). Meanwhile over-zealous recreational hunting quotas in some countries, coupled with the increasing demand for skins, teeth, blood and other body parts in China principally, play an increasing role in declining lion numbers.

Lions, whether in reality or in the abstract, have enthralled us since time immemorial. On our earliest artefacts and temple reliefs the "king of the beasts" has been portrayed as a symbol of power and strength. Rulers from the ancient times – Egyptian, Sumerians, Chinese, Indians, Greeks and Romans, even modern dynasties such as the current British monarchy – have embraced the lion as their royal symbol.

Through the ages the image of a lion has been central to heraldry, and is resplendent on many national flags and coats of arms. Today it is used as an emblem for sports teams and businesses. Any time we wish to express courage and endurance, the image of a lion is usually the first that comes to mind: strong as a lion, proud as a lion, lion hearted, king of the jungle, king of beasts.

So can you imagine an Africa without lions? Not only would we be spiritually impoverished, we would be economically hamstrung too. The lion embodies the very essence of our wild, energised continent. What tourist would want to come to Africa if there were no lions?

There is no doubt that Africa without free-ranging lions would be a misfortune beyond words: future generations might well get to glimpse these magnificent cats only behind the bars of cages or in enclosures. Psychologically, the entire energy of the planet would diminish and so would we, humankind, without the one other species against which we have always found the measure of ourselves. Just ask the lion men.

Leaping Lizards, Predatory Giraffes and Other Game Ranger Myths and Legends

THOSE OF US OF A certain age and bent will recall *Mad* magazine's "silly answers to stupid questions" department. One that sticks in mind is of a ditzy woman with a beehive hairdo, bounding up on tiny high heels, to a lift with a blinking "up" arrow, and asking: "Is this one going up?" The droll man inside wearing a Fifth Avenue suit and trilby hat replies: "No lady, we're going to fool everyone this time and go sideways."

We've all done it, asked some stupid question that's left us feeling small afterwards. Any time we find ourselves out of our element, or out of our culture, or perhaps feeling intimidated and forgetting really basic stuff, we tend to trip over our intellects and ask things like: Why is it so green here (in Ireland)? Or, how come it's raining (in Spain)? Or, who's performing at Piccadilly Circus? Or (and this I find to be an entirely sensible one) where do the people hibernate in winter – in any place where it snows a lot.

I remember an otherwise intelligent friend on her first visit to a game reserve asking the guide: "Are those Bambies?" On any other day you might have given her a field guide, opened to the page with impalas and she would have identified them correctly. But, feeling outside her urban comfort zone, she reached into her deep subconscious for a reference point and pulled out one from a favourite childhood story.

I was once hosting a group of American students, touring southern Africa. One day one of them asked me: "So if Pretoria is the capital of South Africa, what is the capital of Africa?" These were post-graduate students, not kids, in an African Studies programme. I was sorely tempted to have a *Mad* magazine moment and say it was Cairo, the original one.

But those of us who grew up in, or regularly visited, the bushveld tend to be blasé about how much we know about it, or how little first-time visitors from overseas know about our back yard. A classic example of this is the supposed time a giraffe is seen with a bone in its mouth and a guest asks the guide: "Do giraffes hunt in packs?"

Our first instinct might be to laugh, excepting that it's not a silly question at all – if indeed it is more than just a bush fable. Bushwhackers who know their sunis from their dik-diks also know giraffes do on occasion chew on old bones in order to gain a calcium boost. Many people think hippos eat fish, so why not giraffes eating meat?

Speaking of hippos, my hackles rise whenever (and it is rather too often) I hear someone say with much authority: "Did you know, hippos kill more people in Africa than any other animal?"

My first inclination is to give them a flick on the ear. My second is to correct their grammar. What I actually do depends largely on the hour and how many soldiers have fallen. Just how this kind of baloney gets passed around unscrutinised beats me, but I guess you could say this of just about any urban legend or bush myth. Like the one about an apple falling onto Isaac Newton's bewigged head (there's no record of him ever saying one did, only that he thought about it).

If we are talking about large animals, the title holder is undoubtedly the Nile crocodile. Every year these river monsters take women and children from water-side settlements on a regular basis. However, being mere women and children, in mostly remote places, the media never gets alerted. It's only when someone in safariland ends up in hot water that we hear about it.

Certainly, hippos attack people (I know this from personal experience), but not nearly by the order of magnitude the safari grapevine would have us believe. When it comes to vertebrates the biggest killers in Africa will be snakes, particularly those of the Viperidae family, those notorious ambush attackers such as the puffadder or one of the bush adders such as the West African carpet viper.

Of course, all of these pale into insignificance if we compare them to the invertebrates. When it comes to members of the animal kingdom nothing trumps the mosquito. The list of diseases they carry is long and includes of course malaria, but also yellow, dengue, West Nile, zika and Rift Valley, among 20 or so known fevers.

However, the biggest killer (non-human that is) might not be animal, vegetable or even mineral. The prime suspect is amoebiasis, or dysentery, a type of gastroenteritis that kills infants like the plague. It's caused by a microscopic, parasitic, shape-shifting, unicellular organism going by the name *Entamoeba histolytica*. Or it could be the bacteria *Shigella*. Either way, call it bloody diarrhoea to be blunt, and it arises invariably in areas of poor water supply, sanitation and hygiene.

It's hard to pin a number on fatalities from these little thingies (either amoeba or bacteria), but an annual figure given for the so-called developing world is in the multi-millions. A figure for annual deaths in Africa attributed to diarrhoea in 2016[2] was around 1.6 million. So, there's your really big killer and, like a hippo, so easy to avert if you know how. Pardon me the digression, I'm off to wash my hands.

Back to hippos, though, and given that they spend most of the day bobbing in pools, it's little wonder many people assume they would eat fish: in fact, in African folklore they once did, but that's another story. One day while explaining that hippos emerge around dusk to go grazing in surrounding grasslands, a guest once exclaimed: "They have legs!"

Laugh if you will, but there are at least two good reasons why someone might think so. The one above about bobbing all day, and then on a deeper biological level: to which other creature would you think hippos are most closely related? Pigs? No, whales.

The fossil record reveals that over time whales and their ancestors have moved between land and water on several occasions, in different regions of the planet. But whether the hippo is a whale working on its return to the sea, or some kind of whale flexing its back-leg chromosomes is above my pay grade to know or say.

---

[2] CIDRAP: "Diarrhoeal disease rates vary across Africa".

A visitor to the Cape's Whale Coast asked his guide whether whales gave birth on land. Not everyone has seen a whale before, or even the ocean. If they've seen a seal on land, a semi-aquatic mammal, why not a whale? We take for granted the things we know, but I would hate to be left to live off my wits in Siberia or Alaska (where do those people get their vegetables?).

MOST STUPID SAFARI QUESTIONS IN the telling involve American guests, because they are generally so engagingly inquisitive and starry-eyed. However, one of the best and possibly one, with some degree of actual veracity, involves a prototypically restrained English woman.

Having typically disembarked from a late morning transfer flight, new arrivals at a safari camp who have endured the luminous welcoming drink, possibly a short song-and-dance by the gaily garbed staff and have filled in the necessary paper work, are instructed to go and relax in their tent (nowadays much more likely to be a canvas-covered chalet) and then to reconvene at tea time prior to embarking for the sundowner game drive. The routine hardly varies.

What does vary, though (apart from the number of scatter cushions), is the aggregate of goodies. Long gone are the days of just a pre-game-drive tea and rusks. Part of the safari-lodge arms race these days concerns the food, with designer chefs preparing meals of haute cuisine of the kind you would expect to find in top city restaurants.

"Tea" has been elevated to London hotel-style "high tea" where long tables groan under piles of cakes, pasties, petit fours, designer sandwiches, fruit platters, tarts and quiches, maybe even sushi platters. Or something more substantial for the hungry. Just what you need in preparation for the few hours plonked in a vehicle, followed by another feast for dinner on your return. Forgive me, I digress once again: it's one of my pet safari subjects.

Meanwhile, said English lady – real or imagined – arrives for tea and discreetly asks to speak with one of the staff, to report a lizard in her tent. Yes, sure, nothing to worry about madam, she is reassured. Lizards will often find their way into tents in order to hunt insects and moths, but are otherwise completely harmless. There is no end to the parade of geckos, skinks and even agamas in the savanna areas where camps are built. Our lady of the lizard tent goes on her game drive (which, annoyingly, people will call a "safari").

On her return, or shortly thereafter, she is back in the office all terribly sorry to be a bother, but she would really appreciate it if a ranger would come and remove the offending creature. So off they go, the appointed khaki-clad staff member much bemused.

They arrive at the canvas villa and lady points under one of two king-size beds. Said staff member get down on his or her knees, head under the bed frame … when all hell breaks loose: out shoots a one-and-a-half-metre-long monitor lizard with tail lashing like a bullwhip and seems to make a leap at its perceived attacker; intrepid game ranger jumps on bed; lady yells and jumps on chair; lizard dashes around the perimeter of the tent until it finds its way out through the flap, or more likely these days door.

Most safari camps are built overlooking a river or lake where monitors, Africa's largest kind of lizard, hang out in reed beds and riverine bush. They are no Komodo dragons in Africa, but a monitor is fearful enough when cornered and always on the hunt for food. This story is repeated nearly as often as the one about killer hippos. Like all myths, it might actually have happened once and spread from campfire to campfire on the bush telegraph.

Game rangers (usually more correctly game guides, but "ranger" sounds so much more exciting) are usually young, in love with the bush and adventure, often themselves or one another, and the best become famous for telling tall stories. Their jobs and, even more important, their tips depend on it.

There is among this band of brothers and sisters another kind of arms race: to see who can get away with telling their guests the most outlandish tales. The list of really good ones includes saying that windsocks at landing strips are feed bags for giraffes, or that sub-adult hippos begin to develop horns in preparation for becoming rhinos. In areas with baobab trees, where sparrow- and buffalo-weavers like to place their untidy grass nests, guides have been known to tell their rapt punters that it is giraffe fodder, having been placed there by the night staff.

Warthogs come in for a lot of misrepresentation. Often they

are mistaken for rhinos, at great distance one imagines. Since they often live in holes, the question has been posed: do they lay eggs? The same for rhinos, when one's credulity is stretched when imaging why anyone would imagine they might lay eggs. Then again, they are so prehistoric looking, why wouldn't something that looks like a descendant of egg-laying dinosaurs be found incubating around here?

One ranger tale tells the story of stopping at a large termite mound and expounding at length on the amazing architecture and social life of these "white ants", when out comes barrelling a warthog. "Is that a termite?" asks one guest in good faith. Laugh if you will, but for anyone in Africa for the first time it's a valid question (and not confined only to visitors to Africa, let's face it.)

A solid, curious-kid-in-classroom question might be: why don't woodpeckers get headaches, or do they in fact? As far as we know they don't (or they'd stop that infernal hammer-hammer-hammering). What they do have is a unique adaptation for their life of hammering at tree limbs – usually dead ones – to get at the insects and their larvae that have holed up in there.

If you took biology and had the opportunity to dissect a woodpecker's head (do not try this at home!), you would see an exceptionally long tongue that, when withdrawn, wraps itself around the brain case and acts as a rubbery cushion. At the base of the bill, as well as at the base of the tongue, are two areas of spongy bone that also help to absorb shock of, on average, 20 hits a second. There is also only a very small space between brain and skull, allowing for only a minimal amount of cerebrospinal fluid through which to transmit vibrations. But I guess that does not mean they do not get headaches sometimes.

Asking if a cheetah is a leopard and vice versa is commonplace, or in one case, whether cheetah was the South African name for a leopard. I wonder how many of my own country-folk could correctly identify a leopard, cheetah, serval, civet and genet: not all cats granted but all spotted nonetheless. I was once confounded by a guest who kept on asking about "cape", which actually sounded more like "kep". Eventually we came upon some buffaloes and he did a victory jump. "There, look, Cape!"

Is this the same moon as we see, and, why are the stars here upside down, are a symptom of northern hemisphere chauvinism, but can open a window for a discussion on astronomy – or astrology if that's the way things lean. For some reason showing people the Southern Cross for the first time appears to be reason to celebrate. Yes, indeed sir, everything is better here.

But it's not only what people say on safari that can be highly entertaining; what some of them do can be so much more so. Stories of guests wanting to get out of game vehicles to take selfies with animals are legion. One can only assume that many people come to Africa with the notion of fun animals having a great time, singing and dancing *a la The Lion King*. Or that African buffaloes ("Cape!") are the same mellow draught animals as the Asian water species.

Also universal are stories of guests turning up for walks in garish clothing, bright broad-brimmed hats or loud umbrellas. I once hosted two Japanese honeymooners who insisted on going on game drives in the biggest hats you've ever seen, and face masks (this was some decades ago) and rushing to be first on the game-drive vehicle so they could nab the front seats. It took endless negotiations in some fifth language, along with loud protestations of other guests, to sort it out.

The old sayings apply here as much as anywhere: there is always something new out of Africa, along with, there's no such thing as a stupid question. Although sometimes there just aren't enough crayons to explain things, or time, like when someone asks what side the sun sets here.

But my all-time favourite involves a client who wanted to photograph only animals defecating. After two days of stopping for every animal leaving its load, the guide just had to ask. Turned out the guest was planning on renovating his bathroom back home and thought images of animals "shitting in the woods" would be a fun décor theme.

Of ~~Mice~~ Gerbils and ~~Men~~ Boys: Three Lads Go on a Very Big Adventure

DONALD HAD A MAP. It was an old Bechaunaland Department of Surveys map of "The Swamps", as the Okavango Delta used to be known. It had come into his possession via an uncle or granduncle who'd done camel patrols in the Kalahari some time early in the 20th century. Or I think that's what he told us.

"Let's go to The Swamps," Don suggested as we sat around his folks' place one weekend drinking beer. He went inside and came back with the stained and brittle paper chart, which he proceeded to unfurl on a poolside table. He, Jerry[3] and I contemplated it for ages as the two-dimensional sepia plane diffused into dreams of deep and dangerous adventure. We were three teenagers just recently set free from school with more enthusiasm than common sense.

At the time there was a silly war going on somewhere up north so, on leaving school, all white males with two legs and a beating heart had been instructed to turn up at their local recruitment office to be injected, inspected, infected, selected, neglected and detected, as well as succumbing to the dreaded obligatory demopping. And so it was that we found ourselves with six months to kill between school and military service. It would be our last shout at freedom for some time. Who knew if we would return, or if that trip, or the army stint thereafter, would be our last?

---

[3] His name is really Tony but he got the name Jerry on a school geography tour. When he went for a dip in a pan, some of his mates stole his clothes, so he sauntered back into camp (ours was a co-ed school) with his modesty concealed behind a Jerry can.

The map was all the more intriguing and alluring due to its scarcity of actual topo-cadastral detail: mainly broken and faded lines with few labels. Some of those that could be discerned were Thamalakane, Santantadibe, Boro (rivers, or more correctly water channels) and Chiefs, Chitabe and Mombo (islands). The fulcrum of the map, bottom centre, was the frontier outpost of Maun. There were also some bridges as I recall: First Bridge, Second Bridge, Third Bridge. I imagined actual solid structures.

We bid goodbye to our parents. Mine were famously laissez faire. I might as well have said I was off to the Hard Rock Café as the Okavango.

We made plans: sleeping bags – check; fishing rods – check; 10-kg rice – check; box of packet soup – check; cash – check (R20 each, remember it was the mid-1970s). We each also had to pack one secret treat to be revealed as if by magic spell. Donald surprised us one night around the campfire with bread made with one can of beer, a packet of self-raising flour and some salt. I produced a packet of biltong during a slow period when the fish weren't biting. Jerry would hold on to his till right near the end, and he would pay the price.

Our only firm strategy was that we'd catch a train from Johannesburg to Francistown and from there hitch-hike – it was a well traversed route Donald was sure, by cattle trucks – first north and then westwards across the legendary Kalahari wastelands to fabled Maun. Once there we would make a plan. South Africans are good at making a plan.

I cannot recall whom, but it must have been one of the more reliable parents who bought us train tickets from Johannesburg to Francistown on the South African Railways–Rhodesian Railways line, and so began my first truly worldly adventure. We were so inexperienced I can only conclude it was our naivety that allowed us to survive the ordeal.

On reaching Francistown station in the evening, we hefted our backpacks and made for the road out of town. That night we slept in the veld somewhere near Tati Town, a township on the perimeter of Botswana's second largest settlement and its industrial link with both South Africa and Zimbabwe.

Of ~~Mice~~ Gerbils and ~~Men~~ Boys: Three Lads Go on a Very Big Adventure

For most of the following morning we threw stones at targets on the dry expanse of the Tati riverbed, watching donkey carts laden with empty water containers trudging down into the sandy riverbed to wells dug into the bed, then trudging back out again once they'd been filled by children using plastic cups and buckets.

Road traffic was somewhat slower. A few cattle trucks did pass us, both full and empty, but none stopped. I was rather grateful because they all seemed to leak slushy cow effluent. It was mid-morning before a cement truck stopped and invited us to jump aboard on top of a convex load of full cement bags. When you are young and skint, you grab whatever bone you are thrown.

The road from there to Nata back then was still gravel but not too bad, while the sun was shining. When we turned west towards Gweta and the vast expanse of the mysterious – to me at that time – Makgadikgadi Pans, the orange sun was lowering its undercarriage towards the runway-flat horizon.

These pans are the remnant of a once vast, fertile region of wetlands about the size of Switzerland: in fact, very much like the greater Okavango region of today. It is one of the largest salt flats on Earth and, together, the three main pans about equal the size of Bolivia's Salar de Uyuni. The difference is that once every several years or so, heavy thunderstorms inundate the Makgadikgadi's enormity and it suddenly teems with life: mainly huge flocks of birds (gulls, terns, skimmers, flamingoes, pelicans, herons and storks of many kinds), frogs and fish, but also migratory mammals, particularly zebra herds.

The "road" at this point degenerated into a braid work of deeply rutted sand tracks. Since we were now deep in the Kalahari proper, as the sun slowly dissolved in a line of orange-brown winter haze, the air began to chill inversely. The combined effects of fine dust and even finer cement powder had us wheezing. An hour or two along this stretch the cold became near intolerable, but no matter how long or hard we banged on the roof of the cab, the driver and his shotgun rider would not respond. And so the truck bounced along at full speed and so did we. The fragrance of cannabis fumes was notable.

There was nothing left to do but, trying to hold on to our bucking conveyance, put on all our clothes and then wiggle into our sleeping bags. Had they seen us our parents would have been appalled, and this was only the start of things. Sometime in the night I heard Donald shouting for help: Jerry had slid off the cement-bag meniscus and had been saved only by Donald grabbing hold of his bag. The two of us managed to wrestle our bug-eyed mate back onto the truck and from then to daybreak there was no sleep. At some time in the early hours we must have passed Gweta.

Maun international airport at the time consisted of a makeshift control room (no tower) and a gravel runway. The town itself had a few prefab colonial-era buildings, Riley's Hotel made mostly from corrugated iron sheeting, and Kays Garage with its single hand-operated fuel pump. The operator was an old man with only half a face: we were told a hyena had attacked him while he slept in his hut. There was a Standard and a Barclays bank, entered by doors on either side of the same low building. Inside was a single teller behind just the one desk. The public library was a mud-and-thatch hut, leaning askance on mopane poles, the encasing cobwebs indicating that no books had been stamped out for some time.

When we finally disembarked at Maun, after dusting ourselves off as best we could and making like vultures in the warming sun, the immediate plan was to spend a sizeable portion of our limited funds on hot breakfast at Riley's. The mere mention of that name sent imaginary pages out of some old African classic fluttering around my head. A loud American guest was sharing the only other occupied table with his pilot, demanding to know what were the SOP, the ETD and the ETA, while filling his face.

We, on the other hand, had to settle on the roof rack of an already heavily laden Land Rover that bounced us along a jeep track up the east bank of the Thamalakane waterway. They threw us off at Crocodile Camp, former home to the legendary Wilmot crocodile hunting family, but more lately a safari jump-off base. Once ensconced at the campsite (only warm Windhoek Export in a blue can available), we started making more plans.

The Okavango Delta is formed where the Okavango River has been arrested by a set of transverse geological faults. Instead of flowing between eastwards into the Zambezi River (as it would have

Of ~~Mice~~ Gerbils and ~~Men~~ Boys: Three Lads Go on a Very Big Adventure

if they were parallel to the river; and indeed as it once had), it has been diverted south where it spreads out into the Kalahari Basin to create the world's largest inland delta, measuring around 50 000 square kilometres at high water.

This magical wetland, surrounded as it is by the endless, waterless reaches of the Kalahari, is one of the great wildlife refuges in Africa. Just about everything in Africa that grunts and groans, scratches and bites, stings, bellows and basically wants to eat you can be found there. We – or at least I – had barely a clue what we were in for.

In the meantime, we heard there was cold beer to be had at a new place across the swirling Thamalakane. (As anyone who knows the region will attest, the waterway lies dry and sandy for most of the year, until the annual floodwaters arrive from distant Angola in April/May and transform it into a torrent for a month or three, depending, replete with all manner of things that slither and swim.) We swam across. How we managed our gear I have no recall.

One-time hunter Tony Graham, who was building Island Safari Lodge across from Croc Camp at the time, took one look at the three fuzzy-faced youths who emerged from the crocodile-infested river to have a drink at his under-construction bush pub with its generator and refrigerator and … I really have no idea what he thought. He did, however, sell us some beers and then negotiated with a local Bayei boatman named Major to take us into the swamps. In those days it, the wild Delta, reached right down to Maun.

"We don't want to go up the main Boro channel," reckoned our self-appointed leader Don, "it's too busy." He'd never been there before. Tony raised an eyebrow. "We want to go up the Santantadibe Channel." Another raised eyebrow but, for R10 from each of us plus a 10-kilogram bag of mealie meal, Major was willing.

At that time the photographic safari lodge had not yet been invented. Rather, most of northern Botswana, or Ngamiland, was divided into hunting concessions, each with a number of seasonal, temporary hunting camps.

"If we head for Chitabe Island I reckon we have a chance of having the place to ourselves." More raised eyebrows. Even though we were there in the middle of the hunting season we did indeed find the place deserted. It was only after we returned that Graham thought to inform us the place had an over-abundance of lions and was generally avoided by most sane people. Then again Maun and its surrounds has always brimmed with whackos, so who was he to judge?

The outbound journey spent poling upstream was idyllic and revelatory. Major did not have one word of English. Donald and Jerry had picked up a few words of Setswana, like *fisi* (hyena) and *tau* (lion) and *kwena* (crocodile), as well as some local tree names, and continually tried to communicate with Major in knocked-up funakalo. I mostly just sat and gawked at the birds and the beasts and took photos of the passing show with my Kodak Instamatic camera.

Three young men and our poler in a mokoro, one of the dugout canoes that are the public transport of these wetlands, must have been quite a sight to the other Bayei, or river Bushmen, we occasionally encountered. Major would chat with them as they slowed, no doubt passing the time of day and news of up and down river, and shrug or chuckle.

Each day, hour by hour, the channel narrowed, from a broad and swift-flowing river to sinuous passage, wending through reed beds, around low islands fringed with stately riparian trees whose names were all magical words to me – mangosteen and mukwa, jackalberry and knobthorn, ilala palm and sausage tree.

Major, who was noticeably tall for a river Bushman, had the advantage of standing while we sat. He would simply point and his passengers might or might not see what he was seeing. White men cannot jump – certainly not up in a mokoro at any rate.

Lechwe, semi-aquatic antelope, tiptoed across the shallows between islands. Hippos bobbed in the pools (ledibas) where our channel opened out, and bellowed as the boat eased past. Baboons barked, monkeys chattered, fish eagles shrieked and occasionally a large crocodile would slide off a sandbar and disappear. Everywhere there were birds like I had never seen, and could hardly believe could exist, in such multi-coloured profusion.

At one point some bushes blocked the mere metre-wide channel. The passenger sitting point had to grab the branches to pull us through. When the entire bush seemed to move we realised these floating islands of water figs were festooned with emerald-coloured snakes sunning themselves. Major, standing at the back, was nonchalant about it all while the three reclining mzungus, white folks, had to deal with whatever came at the sharp end of the boat. He knew, but we were not yet sure, that they were harmless green bush snakes and not green mambas.

There was no going back. Earlier we'd had to make a very abrupt about-face and detour up a side channel when a hippo jumped into the water just ahead of us and showed us its tonsils. That took us into a channel so narrow the papyrus brushed the boat on both sides.

Through all this Major remained tall, aloof and mostly silent. On the first night out we lads watched as he carefully laid out a double kaross, hung a mosquito net from a tree branch, then made a small fire and cooked his dinner. (Many years later Donald informed me that he had in fact carried a tent from South Africa. However, when he'd seen the elaborate bedding Major had packed in the mokoro, decided we would have use of it.)

We looked at one another, nodded our approval and even started doing the ching-chong-cha routine to determine the head-to-toe arrangement. But then, and without so much as a "good night gentlemen and good luck," Major slipped silently under his net and, with the sun's lids blinking, tucked himself up and immediately nodded off. We on the other hand had to settle for plonking our sleeping bags on the bare ground. He probably thought we were as mad as a bag of snakes.

The next few days were spent in primordial bliss as the daily routine was established: get up with the sun into the chilling June morning air, make some food, then pole for the rest of the morning. Around midday we'd stop on an island and go for a walk with silent Major as guide, or swim in one of the ledibas. We had only the slightest concern for crocodiles.

We were much more concerned about lions, buffaloes and elephants, but in fact we only ever got to see them at a distance. Mosquitoes and tsetse flies, on the other hand, were far more numerous and in our faces. And our backs, our arms and our legs. If ever you have been bitten by a tsetse fly you will not soon forget it. It's like being jabbed with a red-hot needle.

After our midday constitutional we'd pile back into the boat and, for a few idyllic hours, just drift (it felt like drifting, but of course Major was putting in the effort from behind). Once when Donald tried to intimate that he'd like to give the poling lark a try, Major left no room for doubt that it just was not going to happen. Around late afternoon we – or rather our guide – would decide on an island to stop and make camp.

On reaching Chitabe Island, a lovely camping spot was located right next to a big lediba and we spread ourselves out in a grove of big trees and ilala palms, the ones that carry the vegetable ivory fruits, each about the size and consistency of a billiard ball. At sunset Major would erect his envied bivouac while we three lads would each seek out a soft place to lay our beds.

I remember one night as the sun was setting we heard the sound of voices, singing, but from which direction and how far was impossible to determine. Sound carries on the water channels much as they flow with water. Also at that time baboons started barking and screeching in the overhead trees. I learned later the phenomenon is called Hesperian anxiety.[4] It's the time when primates take stock for the night ahead, filled with dark spirits and big-toothed beasts. It's the bear in the cave; the ghost in the cupboard, the tokoloshe under the bed. It's our primordial fear of the dark.

Then we heard lions calling, albeit faintly and from somewhere far off. I was sure they'd find us during the long hours of the night. Later the eerie yelp of hyenas drifted to us from who knew where. Tales of hyenas attacking people, picked up on their previous safari, were recalled around the campfire that night. Being the bush novice and, quite frankly, terrified, I made sure to keep the fire well fed while Jerry and Donald slept.

Some time during the night there was a single "plop". Donald rolled over and shone his torch towards the water and illuminated

---

[4] Hesperian anxiety describes what appears to be a universal fear of the dark displayed by primates, at least those of the African savanna. It was coined by polymath Eugene Marais while studying baboons, and named after the Hesperides, Greek nymphs who were the daughters of the evening.

the dark mass of a herd of buffaloes drinking, knee deep in the lediba. It turned out we'd made camp on a game trail. A single drip had dropped from the lips of one animal; they had made no other sound.

Those most certainly were days of miracle and wonder. We played at safari, walked, stalked animals, watched birds, swam, fished. Over the years I've often reflected on how foolhardy we were but also worn it as a kind of Boy Scouts badge of honour.

Years later when I ran a safari camp in the Delta, I got to see just how shoulder to tail those waterways are crammed with crocodiles. Once an overland safari group stopped at the nearby campsite and some of the German tourists jumped into the channel for an irresistible dip. One of them was never seen again. How we escaped back at Chitabe I can only put down to crocs being essentially shy, the place teeming with fish, or to some river spirit.

The following night I was exhausted from my previous night's vigil and slept deeply. That was the night Jerry needed me most. The two of us had set our bags on one side of the fire with Donald on the far side, next to a fallen ilala log. Dark gave way to gloom.

"Hey, David. David! Daavid!"

"Hmmmm?"

The cold winter sun was just tickling the palm fronds with frosty fingers when his desperately whispered pleas penetrated my wood-smoke-filtered dreams.

"I've been trying to wake you for hours. I think there is a snake in my sleeping bag."

"What kind?"

"How the hell do I know what kind! It was dark. It's crawled all the way down to my feet."

The first thought that comes to everyone's mind in the Okavango whenever "snake" is mentioned is black mamba – most dreaded of all snakes in Africa. It was a mamba that had killed legendary crocodile hunter Bobby Wilmot. Bit him on the bum when he stepped over a log not far from Chitabe.

With this very much in mind I realised I was going to need some back-up. But Donald, never one in love with the dawn, was not easily roused. I started pelting him with vegetable ivory fruits and when one hit him on the head his second remark, after having vowed to kill me, was: "How big is it?"

"I don't bloody know! My whole body is numb. I wouldn't be surprised if it's already bitten me," shout-whispered our stricken friend.

We, the other two, were equally surprised. It was the longest outburst we'd ever heard from Jerry.

"C'mon okes, do something, quickly!"

Don and I agreed, in the interest of our own collective survival, to put aside our current squabble and help our prostate comrade. It took considerable minutes of heated debate to formulate a plan. Jerry's numb body was not going to be of much assistance and Donald's plan of dumping hot coals on his sleeping bag was vetoed.

First it had to be assumed the snake was of the dangerous sort and would not much appreciate being disturbed from its warm slumber on a cold winter's morning. It was finally decided that, given the victim's uncooperative anatomy, and given that we were in Big Snake country, a bold and daring move was essential.

I would grab hold of the bottom two corners of the sleeping bag (very carefully, Jerry insisted), while Donald would get hold of the feverish victim by his armpits. On the count of three we would yank hard in opposite directions and hope for the best.

"One, twoo, …"

"Hold on okes! Let's go over the plan again," a sweating Jerry implored. He needed more time to visualise the move and confront his worst reptilian nightmare.

Several countdowns later, "one, twooooo, THREE!" we shouted and jerked as hard and as fast as we could. Jerry fell in a useless pile on top of Donald while I was left holding the sleeping bag by its tips. Donald picked up a stick from our woodpile while I gingerly upended the bag and gave it a shake.

What happened next happened quickly. Something dropped out and Donald took a swipe at it. In the confusion the heavy stick cracked down on my hand and I hopped away yelling in pain. Donald fell on the dusty ground in a paroxysm of laughter and Jerry found himself staring eyeball to eyeball into the terrified face of a matchbox-sized creature sitting on elongated hind legs, its diminutive front paws wiping its twitching, whiskered snout.

That evening I sported a makeshift splint around my left hand while Jerry was showing welts from where we'd pelted him with vegetable ivories after he revealed his special treat as a celebration. He hadn't realised a tin of baked beans would not be everyone's idea of a treat.

Tatera leucogaster, a bushveld gerbil, we agreed afterwards, poring over a field guide back at Island Safari Lodge. Donald still insists he never meant to break my fingers, but I've never been convinced. While sitting quaffing cold beers, someone asked us where we'd been.

Chitabe Island we answered in unison.

No one goes there these days, we were informed. Too many lions.

For my next birthday I asked my parents to please gift me a copy of *Roberts* and a pair of binoculars.

Antelope and Evolution: When Whales Walked, Giraffes had Short Necks and WTF is a Gerenuk Anyway?

IN THE CLANDESTINE CULT OF sub-editors, of which I was once briefly a paid-up member, there exists an award so secret it is acknowledged only by winks and nods: it's known as the Headline Award. Possibly the all-time best-ever contender was coined in 1986 when British Labour MP Michael Foot was elected to chair a nuclear disarmament organisation. *The Times* of London ran with "Foot Heads Arms Body".

When I was working at *Getaway* magazine we had a nominee, for a story about the wildlife of the northern Kenya reserves: "What the Fuck is a Gerenuk?" It was thought up by the art director but, alas, never made it into print (apparently we were a family magazine). Nevertheless he had a very good point. What the heck is a gereneck … ooops, there's a Darwinian slip right there.

The gerenuk of the dry regions of northern Kenya and Somalia is one very strange beastie indeed, looking something like the progeny an antelope and a giraffe might have: an intermediate species, in evo-speak. There was quite a lot of evo-arguing in our household, principally between my very smart Catholic father and me. His favourite riposte was: "Show me the intermediate species; where's the missing link?"

Like so many family affairs it was an impossible argument, not least being the subtle point that evolution doesn't really work that way. Like the famous missing link between humans and primates: everyone wants to see *the* missing link. There isn't one, but there are several hominid links you can place along the evolutionary continuum from monkey to you. What there is, or are, are common ancestors from which we split and split and split. What we do share with monkeys is a common ancestor, a proto-monkey that lived around 14 million years ago (mya).

At Oxford University back in 1860 the town was astir, anticipating what was billed to be the Great Evolution Debate. Darwin himself declined to attend (he was a sickly old man by then), so it was left for Bishop Samuel Wilberforce to enquire of "Darwin's bulldog", Thomas Henry Huxley, whether he was a monkey on his mother's or his father's side. That brought down the house, but today we know a whole lot more about how evolution works, especially in the area of genetics.

In my own "great domestic debate" the gerenuk became my poster species for intermediate types. It's hard to explain any other way, this antelope that has a body which looks like any other gazelle, but whose neck appears as if it's spent all its spare time playing "Stretch Guy"[5] with the Nubian giraffes with which it shares a habitat.

In fact, there's another similar species of East Africa, the dibatag. You'd be hard pressed to tell them apart in the very dry places where their ranges overlap on the Horn of Africa. It's the horns: male gerenuks have heavier, impala-like horns, while dibatags have shorter, lighter, more reedbuck-like ones.

What they are, rather than being any intermediates between antelopes and giraffes, are examples of extreme environmental adaptation among one of the most successful of all mammal groups, the African antelope. There are 91 species split into 30 genera.

Darwin was a very smart man and he observed the workings of nature on so many levels; there's never been another naturalist quite like him (other than, arguably, Alexander von Humboldt). Anyway, the Englishman noted how, if you placed all the individuals of one species in a long row, the most extreme at either end would resemble more closely other related species than one another. An alien visitor introduced to a 2.2-metre-tall Scandinavian and a bow-legged, 1.5-metre Pygmy could be excused thinking they were different species.

---

[5] "Stretch Guy" is a Google Play device app.

That would be as confusing as, say, a novice game watcher trying to tell apart a thin puku from a fat lechwe in the Chobe or Luangwa areas where their distributions overlap. Never mind a gerenuk and a dibatag. Or a beginner twitcher with the larks, or the warblers, or the raptors, especially the brown eagles (the juveniles have even the binocular and notebook squad all a-twitter).

The antelope have been described as being a "wastebasket taxon" in the family Bovidae, even-toed ungulates: basically everything that is not buffalo, sheep, goat or cattle. Just think about them, from the tiny dik-dik weighing in at around 1.5 kilograms, to a giant eland of up to 1 tonne.

Whenever my dear departed father threw down his "show me the intermediate species" card, I would rattle off my bokkie litany: Dik-dik, suni, steenbok, grysbok, klipspringer, oribi, springbok, impala, lechwe, puku, waterbuck (two species), sitatunga, nyala, kudu … dramatic breath … reedbuck (two species), rhebuck, bushbuck, tsessebe, hartebeest, blesbok, bontebok, sable, roan, oryx, wildebeest (two species), eland. And that's just in southern Africa, not counting the 22 species of duiker. How many more would you like?

While I'd watch him mulling that over, I'd pull out my two aces and slam them down on the negotiating table: Gerenuk, slam! Dibatag, dunk! I could also have used my pack of monkeys, of which there are 111 species found in Africa alone, excepting that would lead to the overwhelming question of whether we were monkeys on his mother's or his father's side. Not to mention the wag-'n-bietjie wrangle over extinct hominids; the antelope offered an easier game.

Hoo boy! there's nothing quite so monkey-like as an evolutionary denialist who won't be hearing no evil. When they throw out their bomb blanket "yes, but it's just a theory", you want to swat them with your prized copy of *On the Origin of Species*.

Actually, it's best to ignore them and save yourself all kinds of trouble. They probably wouldn't have a clue anyway that there are two very different kinds of theory when it comes to describing nature, the universe and everything (as opposed to say laws, ethics or religious affinity).

The first is called an un-scientific theory, in which there is an idea that might well be a good one, but has not yet been, or cannot be, proven. An example of this would have been the theory of continental drift prior to 1970. Up until that time it was an idea proposed by some geologists to explain why the rocks in locations far removed on Earth appeared to be all but identical. Many people in geological circles pooh-poohed it: "Show us the proof; that's just a theory," they bayed.

The proof came in the early 1970s when fossil bones of an extinct species of a type of dinosaur, well known from the rocks of the Karoo Supergroup in central South Africa, were found in the Kitching Mountain range in Antarctica. There was only one way that could have occurred: the two landmasses had to have been connected at the time that species lived (a blunt-tusked mammal precursor named *Thrinaxodon*, around 250 mya).

This "unscientific" theory was immediately elevated to the second kind – a full scientific theory and no one bothers any longer to debate it. Since that time, the number of fossil species found that occur in now-separated regions of the world are as the grains in a sandpit, such has been the flourishing in the discipline of palaeontology over the past 50 years or so.

For some people theories such as the "big bang" remain in the realm of the un-scientific, but those are people who themselves remain in the medieval mindset (not without good reason also known as the Dark Ages). The same applies now to evolution, which, until well into the 20th century was, like continental drift, considered by many still to be a good-guess theory but not unequivocally proven, or "scientific". Genetic DNA analysis can now pinpoint what or who came from where, and even when.

The way real scientists look to prove a theory is first to try to disprove it. Just one piece of irrefutable evidence that a cosmic big bang did not occur around 14 billion years ago would disprove it and we'd have to move on to some new theory: like there was no beginning, it's always been there.

When it comes to evolution, the evidence in favour lies mainly in two areas of scientific endeavour: the first is the fossil record, and the second, modern genetics. There exist today many millions of fossils of organisms that lived in times past but that are now extinct. By recording in which geological strata they occur, the age and sequence of that layer, one can create a vast "family tree" of all the things with bodies that will mineralise under the right conditions, known to have lived on Earth. If one, just one, single fossil was found out of sequence, the theory would immediately be disproved. But none has to date.

One could argue that the absence of this one specimen does not mean it does not exist. Indeed, the absence of evidence cannot be said to be evidence of the absence. But one single hypothetical case to disprove the theory, stacked against the innumerable millions of known ones: you'd have to be a very blind monkey to not see, or want to see, which way the chips are stacked.

Back to my own Great Debate about Darwin's theory of "the tendency for species to form varieties, and on the perpetuation of varieties and species by natural means of selection". I could have mentioned the green pigeon, half-dove and half-parrot, or the lammergeier vulture that is half eagle. Or pythons, which have spurs that are vestigial leg bones, alongside legless skinks. There's some considerable intermediary-form wiggle room right there.

I wish I'd known more about the lineage of whales back then. For example, did you know, the closest living relative to modern whales is the hippo? All living whales have vestigial back leg bones, and even the dead ones, which you can see clearly in the displays of the Whale Well at the Iziko South African Natural History Museum in Cape Town.

It's common sense that, being mammals, whales are descended from some land animal. That creature is, or was, *Pakicetus attocki*, an animal that had the body of a large hyena-wolf, but with a very whale-like skull. It lived in the area that is now the border between India and Pakistan, around 50 mya, close to water, and ate mainly fish.

The first well documented information about very old whales comes from the American Midwest, when pioneer farmers began ploughing up excessive numbers of large, round, drum-like fossil bones. They were used for all manner of things from cornerstones to farm boundary markers, and in fact became so numerous and irksome to the farmers, most were simply discarded.

However, in 1832, an Arkansas farmer decided that the sequence of 28 large contiguous bone-rocks might be of interest to the smart folks of the American Philosophical Society in Philadelphia. They were, but no one there really had a clue what they were, other than that it was noticed some of the sediment that came with them contained seashells.

Not long after that another landowner sent more fossilised bones, this time including skull, jaws, forelimbs, vertebrae and ribs. The Society's leading naturalist, Richard Harlan, thought they might be from a kind of long extinct creature that was known at the time, the marine plesiosaur – a kind of lizard-turtle-shark.

Harlan named it *Basilosaurus* (king lizard). He took his giant "lizard" to show in London, at that time the centre of the English-speaking scientific world. It was there that the rising star of anatomy, Richard Owen, recognised it as being a mammal: but what kind? While on the road show in England a bone from inside the skull dropped out: it was identical to the inner ear bones of modern whales.

That was pretty much as far as whale palaeontology went until the discovery of *Pakicetus* a century and a half later, in 1981. However, starting in the 1990s, the fossil remains of other archaeocetes (marine whale ancestors) were uncovered in both Pakistan and India, at what one cetologist described as "a dizzying pace". The seven taxa found to date – *Pakicetus, Himalayacetus, Ambulocetus, Remingtonocetus, Kutchicetus, Rodhocets* and *Maiacetus* – elegantly describe the early evolution of whales. So, there they are right there, as many intermediate types at which you'd want to shake a dead monkey.

But bear in mind, these are only the ones that have been found to date. What many people don't get is how hard, and rare, it is to find a fossil intact. These are creatures with hard parts that died in some soft substrate, sand or mud, did not get broken up, eaten or otherwise destroyed or fragmented, and lay there under increasing loads of sediment.

Over many years the bone material was infiltrated by water and slowly metamorphosed to mineral. Typically, it would be covered by successive layers of sediment over millions, tens of millions, maybe hundreds of millions of years, which all turned to rock. Then that rock had to erode down again, over hundreds of millions, tens of millions of years, so that a human walking in the veld would find it on or close to the current surface. Finding fossils can be a one in a million, or ten million, or hundred million roll of the dice.

I wish I had known about the West Coast Fossil Park when my father was still around. We could have taken a drive out into the country one day, done some bird watching at Langebaan, then driven down to Langebaanweg to stand and stare at the fossils of creatures that lived there between five and three million years ago.

You can stand on platforms and look at the actual fossils of creatures that lived and died in an ancient course of the Berg River: there are four-tusked elephants, giant buffaloes and giant hyenas, a huge African bear – twice as large at least as modern polar bears, numerous aquatic species and a giant, short-necked giraffe.

"See Dad," I'd point, "there's your intermediate species."

"Pah!" he'd scoff, and chuckle disdainfully.

"Let's go for tea and scones back at the Geelbek Restaurant in the national park," I'd cajole, happy for his company.

Goggas and the Veld Tool Box

THAT CLASSIC MONTY PYTHON PARODY on the Sunday School favourite, *All Things Bright and Beautiful* ("All things dull and ugly") is so funny because it is also true about each little snake that poisons and each little wasp that stings (He made their brutish venom, He made their horrid wings. Amen).

It goes to the very nature of creation: you cannot credit him, her or it with making butterflies and song birds unless you also praise same for "all things scabbed and ulcerous, all pox great and small". It is much easier to see only the "bright and beautiful" side of creation if you've grown up on an English country estate. But I'm betting your version of an almighty will be quite different if you grew up in a tropical rainforest or the African bush.

Who, after all, made all the snakes and spiders, the wasps and the bees, not to mention Aids and Ebola, malaria and amoebic dysentery? I have to admit, it's long floored me why a gaboon viper would be gifted the biggest fangs in the family of snakes, with among the largest venom glands filled with extremely virulent cytotoxin, in order to overcome its principal food – mice. Not everyone does, but I have a singular interest in them and their kind, as well as all the things we might call goggas.

It's such a lovely word that, *gogga*. It can refer to something creepy and crawling, or it be used as an endearment: "my lovely little gogga you!" It's one of only a few Khoi and San words that have found their way into the grand lexicon of Sefricanisms. Others include kwagga, buchu, dagga, kaross, kierie, einah! (always an exclamation) and aitsa, which means sweet, as in lekker. It would be really lekker if there were more of them. What there is no shortage of, though, is actual goggas.

We are all familiar with the now-tired observation about the abundance of beetles in the universe. There are an estimated 600 000 known species worldwide; the problem is counting them, because every time someone starts looking with scientific intent in a new place, lots of new Coleoptera pop out. Of insects as a whole, there are about a million known, and thought to be up to ten times that still unknown.

How many actual individual beetles there are no one seems able to say, although estimates on the number of individual ants (a paltry 14 000 to 20 000-odd species) puts it at around 10 000 trillion of the little scurriers. In Southern Africa we have about 550 recorded species of ants, compared to around 18 000 species of beetles. But there'll be many more ants because typically they live in large colonies, some of which can be extremely populous, whereas beetles are much less sociable.

I remember learning that the entire biomass of all mammals of the African savanna does not come close to that of the termites underground there. We know them mostly when they come out as flying ants, or alates, and who did not run out at dusk and swat them with tennis rackets, or collect them in baskets to deep fry in palm-nut oil, depending on where you lived?

Talking of delicacies, one of this region's bonanzas is the great big springtime worm eruption. Wherever mopane trees grow (the Lowveld, the Limpopo and Zambezi valleys and across to the Okavango) there you'll find the emperor moth *Gonimbrasia belina*, and where you find it you'll find its eggs, a few months later (midsummer), you will hardly be able to miss the fifth stage of its larval form, a caterpillar otherwise known as the famed mopane worm. I've been in the Kruger National Park when you could barely move but for crunching them underfoot.

These juicy, brightly coloured, thumb-sized "worms" are eaten by a host of birds, and humans too. Fresh is the main delicacy, but they are also dried or smoked for year-round consumption and form an important source of protein for people of the mopane belt. In spaza shops in Venda I've seen dry worms piled in grass baskets and offered to schoolchildren as "change", as elsewhere they might be given bubblegum.

They are so important economically, people will lay claim to patches of mopane trees and harvest the worms for sale in a hotly contested market. Stealing worms in the dark of night is rife during the worm season. The yield in South Africa alone is around 1.6 tonnes annually, netting many millions of rands. You'll even find them canned in some areas.

We all know what a gogga is – basically anything small that creeps, crawls or flies without benefit of feathers. Cockroaches are goggas, as are ants and termites – basically all insects and their allies. Millipedes and centipedes are definitely goggas, but slugs and snails, as well as snakes – things that slither and slide – tend not to be.

Arachnids most definitely are: scorpions and spiders, basically, but also stuff like ticks and mites, collembola, diplura and protura – the kinds of things you'd look at under a microscope and get the flibberty-jibbers. Some other better-known groups include mayflies, damselflies and dragonflies, another mantids and stick insects, earwigs (an unexpectedly large group), grasshoppers and the like, and zoraptera (I don't know either but apparently things like thrips and psocids).

Some of the less well-liked sorts include cockroaches and lice, also fleas and flies, and then some of the even lesser known but more interesting ones like antlions and lacewings (larval and adult forms respectively), stoneflies, caddisflies and scorpionflies (imagine one of them landing in your soup!) and then the ones we know and (mostly) love – the moths and butterflies, bees and wasps.

KIDS LIKE TO COLLECT STUFF. When we were young we kept all manner of things at home and sometimes took them to school to show our friends. You could rely on Brian having a velvet mole or a cute little hedgehog in his blazer pocket. Bert was an extreme collector and if you visited his place you might find a puffadder asleep in his jersey drawer, or a baby jackal under his bed. His mother had no idea that some of these things might be dangerous and one day arrived home with a rinkhals on the back seat of her Cortina. "I've got something for you Bert," she announced in her delightfully thick Dutch accent.

Up on the Highveld we did not have the big five so busied ourselves with the little – admittedly it was only four because we did not have buffalo weavers. But we did look for elephant shrews in old termite mounds, dig for antlions with grass stalks, let leopard tortoises roam in our gardens and try to goad rhino beetles into battle. Some of the little critters we handled were much more dangerous than we realised, like the night adders and stiletto snakes we sometimes kept. But that's kids for you. Thinking back, our lunch boxes were like our tool boxes, often filled with things that not only crept or crawled, but also stung and bit as well.

Blister beetles, Matabele ants, scorpions and baboon spiders were among the bigger hitters in our veld tool kits. Luckily no one we knew was ever seriously stung or otherwise envenomed by any of them because the consequences could have been serious indeed. Take the stiletto snake for example: it looks very much like an innocuous black worm snake but has side-action fangs which can inject a potent dose of venom that has caused the complete loss of fingers for some unlucky handlers. The snake delivers a cocktail of neuro- and cytotoxins, eliciting intense pain, which is followed by tissue necrosis against which antivenom is no use. If you try to pick one up, chances are it will give you a sideways zap. The things our moms didn't know about!

Most blister beetles are easy to spot, being black with vivid yellow, red or orange spots on their backs. Generally, leave them alone because, although they cannot bite or sting, they can excrete a nasty toxin called cantharidin that will cause bad welts or blisters. They tend to hang around bright flowers, looking for bees to parasitise. Horses have been known to experience severe poisoning from them when feeding on alfalfa in fields where they have massed, and even once it's been harvested.

For the children who lived along our river a special spanner was an African water bug, evidence of its presence being much more common than the thing itself. Measuring in at 10–12 centimetres it's a real whopper and hard to beat in a tool-measuring contest. That's a gogga about the size of a bar of soap, and it's a flying, biting one. They are inclined to lurk at the bottom of muddy and weedy backwaters, waiting to pounce on a passing fingerling, tadpole or frog; the larger ones even grab crabs, baby terrapins or small water snakes.

They strike at passing prey with their front legs, which are adapted to what the textbooks describe as "raptorial appendages". Once in the bug's grasp, the unfortunate prey is pierced with a needle-like proboscis and injected with saliva containing powerful dissolving enzymes. The bug then sucks out its insides and casts aside the shrivelled skin. Whenever you see a deflated, dried out frog skin you can bet it was the victim of a toe biter.

Those raptorial appendages can inflict a gash in your hand should you pick one up, or on a toe if you tread on one in the water, but it's not any more serious. It looks like a very giant aquatic cockroach, but actually it cannot breathe underwater.

The bugs have two special SCUBA adaptations that allow them envied bottom time. The first are two hollow half-tubes that can be extended out of what you could only call its bum and, when joined, form a tube which they use as a snorkel. The other is a hollow between their backs and wings where they can store an air bubble. Out of the same place where the snorkel protrudes, they can also eject a really foul smelling fluid. It's best to leave them be.

Giant water bugs are super impressive for sure, but when the tape measures come out the winners will always be stick insects (Phasmatodea, all strictly vegetarians and entirely harmless). I thought the one I found in the Kalahari, and measured at 25 centimatres when fully outstretched, was a real whopper. I fancy it was a Southern African giant stick insect *Bactrododema tiaratum*. Not everyone around the campfire was as impressed with it as I, but that's entomophobiacs for you.

They might be comforted to know that much larger ones are found elsewhere, the longest of all being females of the genus *Phryganistria* found in south-east Asia (where you'll find them deep fried at most street and floating markets). They can tip the tapes at 60 centimetres. By comparison the largest in Southern Africa is a newly described species from the Kruger National Park, *Bactrododema krugeri*, the type specimen of which measured 30 centimetres with legs outstretched front and back.

Looking similar but not very closely related to the stick insects are the praying mantises or, more correctly, mantids (Mantodea, which are all carnivores). But possibly their most engrossing characteristic is their deviant sexual behaviour. The one we know most about is that female mantids bite off their mates' heads during or just after copulation.

We knew about this when we were young and were titillated by the idea, but in fact we didn't know the half of it. We also knew that some spiders practised this head-eating thing. What we did not know was just what a fierce arms-and-legs race it was out there. For example, in some spider species the males have learned to first tie up their partners, or to arrive laden with gifts that keep her busy while he is on the job.

That it is done at all is surprising enough, but why is even more so. People who watch these things have seen stick insect and mantid couples mating seemingly continuously for weeks at a time. They say it is likely to be that the male is trying to ensure no other males get to his mate before he's sure his sperm has fertilised her eggs.

At least in the case of mantids it seems that as soon as the male loses his head, his body goes into paroxysms of sexual frenzy. We don't want to over anthropomorphise this, but on appearance it would seem to be a strong incentive for the female.

When young we fooled around with dung beetles mainly because they are so large and some of them – like the rhino beetles – irresistible looking. And also because young people just cannot help themselves when it comes to matters scatological. What it took beetle scientists to work out, however, was the complex sexual conduct among some males, known as the "big balls" phenomenon (it seems to apply right across the animal kingdom). The lesson here is that size does count big time when it comes to females of a species selecting a male with which to mate.

Among antelope, deer, moose, elk, bison and all their kind it is much more obvious and plenty of studies have shown that horn or antler size is a major determinant in mating success. As it is among horned dung beetles. Males with the biggest horns get to mate with what we must presume are the hottest female dung beetles. Actual copulation has not been observed very often, but when it has it's been noted that they do it mainly while tunnel digging: at regular intervals the male mounts the female from behind, grabs her with his two front legs and as his body goes into spasms he taps intently on her carapace.

Later, while she is busy laying eggs down the burrow, he hangs around the entrance to make sure no other males get any action with his female. Or that's what he thinks. The moment his attention is diverted, or he wanders off even a small distance, smaller-horned rivals will race down the burrow and copulate with the female. Some will even dig their own burrows to intersect with hers and sneak in that way. Needless to say, they are labelled "sneaks" by coleopterologists.

Some crickets have developed an ingenious method of catching a mate. The males of some field cricket species, ones that mate with the female on top, have a parallel set of toothed ridges down their backs. If a female climbs atop a male he can seize her in his armed snare and force her to copulate.

Mites are something else altogether and they are pretty much all parasites. If you looked carefully enough, you'd find them in all the moist parts of your body including armpits, your groin, on your scalp and eyelashes, even floating around on your eyeballs. Some we call ticks, but the majority are smaller than a millimetre and look like the most fearsome creatures you – or George Lucas – could dream up: like his brain worms in *The Clone Wars*.

The female of one variety of mite (and there are thousands) sucks out the soft insides of mealworm beetle eggs. Newly developed and already fertilised female mites will latch on to the underside of a mealworm beetle and wait for it to lay its eggs. She bites into an egg, much bigger than herself, and then, as with most soft-bodied ticks, sucks it until her body size swells enormously, relatively speaking (as much as 20 times her original size). She then drops off and her own eggs develop inside her.

When they hatch the males fertilise the females – technically their sisters – which causes the mother's body to burst. While the fertilised female offspring wander off in search of a mealworm beetle, the males – which have only rudimentary legs – are mostly left trapped inside their mother's body and die there, or not far from it.

In ancient Egypt, as well as prehistoric Inca and Hawaiian

societies, the ruling classes procreated only with their own siblings. The reasoning was that they were divine and so gods could only reproduce with other gods, and not mere mortals. Problems invariably arose with recessive genes (which come in the form a double dose from the father) that enfeebled the family lineage. This problem does not apply to insects, which have what is known as "paternal genome elimination", whereby recessive male genes are destroyed at embryo stage.

The more you seek, the weirder it gets down among the grass stalks and flowers. Consider the male spider, which has not one but two penises, one on each side of its mouth, called pedipalps. The female has two genital openings on the underside of her thorax.

Some male spiders avoid sexual oblivion by using spurs on their legs, which they jam into the female's jaws, while others tie up their partners with webbing. Males of some spider species even secrete a kind of intoxicating liquid from special horns, which allows them to get off unscathed.

In nature there is hardly any kind of sexual behaviour that has not been recorded – for example homosexuality is rife, from bottlenose dolphins to baboons, as much as from penguins to puffins. Male dolphins have a hook at the end of their penises and have been observed using them to hook onto or into the soft parts of not only other male dolphins but also turtles, sharks and eels.

Polyandry is much more common in the animal kingdom than either monogamy or polygamy, especially with birds. Both necrophilia and necrophagia are much more the norm than the exception. Mere incest hardly warrants a wink or a nod in the realm of creepy crawlies. It turns out that we humans are the dull exception when it comes to sexual behaviour.

You might dismiss midges, or gnats (small flies), as being merely irritating pests that buzz around our heads and sometimes get up our noses when we are braaiing or fishing. But they'd surprise you if you could catch – and see – them in the act of procreation (although it's true some are downright dangerous and carry confounding diseases, including African horse sickness).

While copulating, the female surreptitiously pokes her needle-like proboscis into her lover's head, injects a dissolving saliva then sucks out his brains (such as they are) along with his innards. When the male keels over, his genitalia break off inside her. There are some good reasons not to want to be a male midge. You would far rather choose to be a male bee, otherwise known as a drone.

Drones do very little but lie about, eat honey and wait for a maybe once-in-a-lifetime chance to mate with the queen. Typically, there only 40 or 50 drones in an average honeybee colony of around 40 000 little honey-makers. The other 39 950 are females that do all the work, including cleaning the hive (domesticated honeybees) or nest (wild ones), caring for and feeding the young larvae, building the honeycomb, dealing with enemies, warming the hive by vibrating their bodies when it's cold, or fanning it with their wings when it's hot, going out scouting for forage, and collecting pollen for honey and plant resins to make propolis (sticky tar-like stuff that is used as a sealant) ... there's just no let-up for a honeybee.

Female wasps, as many of us well know, are a whole lot more assertive, with some species even practising "male stuffing": a kind of locker room escapade carried out by the worker females. It seems to happen when a female arrives back at the nest with food and pounces on a layabout male who is hovering around hoping for a free meal. She grabs him and stuffs him into an empty brood cell, and will even kick and bite him if he tries to escape. Once the food has been distributed to others, he'll be left to extricate himself, battered and bruised.

SPIDERS ARE UP THERE IN a "scariest creatures in all of goggadom" contest, but they are by no means the winners, as anyone who has come camera-eye to compound-eye with a spider-hunting wasp would concur. You might have seen one, if unknowingly, when a female is digging her brood chamber and you notice a spray of sand particles showering out of the hole. Once excavated you can walk over the entrance, drive cattle or your 4x4 over it: the wasp will return and unerringly find the spot and with one frenzied burst uncover her nuptial chamber.

Otherwise, you might have uncovered its rather splendid little larval balls when digging in your veggie patch. They are usually buried about 15 centimetres underground and are perfect spheres coated in sand grains; they look so good you might imagine they were little bush truffles. The little black spots are vents through which the larvae breathe. Just about everything they do is done at a frenzied speed, not least when the large female races around on the ground looking for spider prey. At least in this case it's usually a fair fight, because they are not scared of taking on spiders substantially larger than themselves.

A baboon spider would be among the big spanners in anyone's veld tool box, and anyone who would allow it to walk on them is guaranteed immediate warrior status. I thought there was nothing to best these hairy, hand-sized arachnids until the day I saw a wasp with an elongated, mostly black body about 5-centimetres long, immobilise a baboon spider with two deft stabs: the first one to the head and the second to the underside of its thorax.

It would have been a female of the family Pompilidae, identified not only by its large size, but also its antennae which curl inwards, and its long legs on which it scurries around while on the hunt. The wasp does not kill the spider, but has a poison that paralyses it. The prey is then dragged down a breeding tunnel and the wasp lays her egg, or eggs, depending on the species of wasp and the size of the prey, in its body. When a wasp egg hatches it has a ready fresh meal on hand, or wing.

I was even more impressed, in the worst way, the time I picked one up and it zapped me on the finger. I would put that experience up at number 4 on the Schmidt scale. Like the Scoville scale (named after its creator, American pharmacist Wilbur Scoville) that measures the bite of a chilli, the Schmidt pain index is named after its creator, American entomologist Justin Schmidt, who studies (and samples) the defence behaviour and armouries of insects.

Since first published in 1983, the crazy guy has refined the scale several times. Originally his five-point scale looked something like this:

0 – ineffective, most small biting ants;

1 – fire ant, small bees ("slight pain, almost pleasant");

2 – honeybee sting (African and Asian honey bees), duration of pain 5–10 mins;

3 – most wasps such as velvet ant, paper wasps and yellowjackets;

4 – bullet ant *Paropanera clavata* found in Central-South American rainforests ("pure, intense, brilliant pain, like walking over flaming charcoal with a three-inch nail embedded in your heel").[6] In its home range it is known as hormiga veinticuatro, the 24-hour ant, because the severe pain lasts a full day.

In the latest revision, the man who knows more about pain than just about anyone since the Spanish Inquisition packed away its toys, added to level 4 the tarantula hawk *Pepsis* sp., a wasp from Central South America very like our own baboon-spider hunting wasps ("blinding, fierce, shockingly electric"), and the warrior wasp *Synoeca septentrionalis* ("torture"), also from the tropical Americas. The bullet ant was pushed up to a new top category, namely 4+.

For his pains, in 2015 Schmidt was awarded an Ig Noble prize in Physiology and Entomology. The *Annals of Improbable Research* magazine, in conjunction with Harvard University, gives this award "to celebrate scientific research that first makes people laugh, and then makes them think". You'd think Schmidt would know better.

Best to not try any of this at home.

---

[6] Natural History Museum, "The Schmidt Pain Index", https://www.nhm.ac.uk/scroller-schmidt-painscale/#15.

Elephants: Pachyderm Proceedings with Some Very Bulky Parts

For much of our colonial period Southern Africa was the largest supplier of ivory to the world. Once Trekboers had opened up the Great Karoo and Garden Route, thence on to Addo and the Eastern Cape beyond, the thunder of muskets echoed across the plains, through the valleys and were muffled in the forests wherever elephant were found.

Although seldom seen in numbers anywhere around modern-day Cape Town, the nearby valley now known as Franschhoek had previously been called Olifantshoek. The modern pass that winds over the folded mountains into the Overberg region is built on the tracks created by the scuffing of elephant feet over millennia. In fact, just about every pass in the Cape was surveyed along elephant migratory routes; otherwise they were paths created by San hunter-gatherers.

First Trekboers, then dedicated ivory hunters and finally agrarian settlers pretty much did for elephants what they had already done for the blue buck, quagga, rhino and buffalo of the region. By the start of the 20th century, the last place in the old Cape colonial region left with a sizeable elephant population was the area known as Addo Bush.

The natural vegetation there is mostly valley bushveld, a kind of bushveld succulent forest replete with spikes and thorns, very dense and tangled, and in some places virtually impenetrable. Even seasoned marksmen proclaimed the place to be a "hunter's hell" and would not venture in too deep.

The modern story of the Addo elephants is inextricably linked to oranges. Until fairly recently, no visitors to the Addo national park were allowed to bring in any of the fruit – on pain of death by elephant. This citrus story begins with one James Kirkwood who, in the 1870s, thought he could make a fortune growing irrigated citrus in the Sundays River valley – the linear oasis of Addo. But so tough did he find the task when he died in 1899 he was bankrupt and "a broken man".

However, it was around the small settlement named after him that the first successful irrigated citrus venture took root, on a 3 000-hectare patch of river frontage. The end of the First World War ushered in a new era of mechanised agriculture and, based on the small success at Kirkwood, farmers named Hume and Babcock copied that example and formed the Addo Land and Irrigation Company.

After the end of the Great War, Afrikaans-speaking farmers moved from failing ostrich farms in the Little Karoo to Kirkwood while, under the stewardship of Percy Fitzpatrick, returning English-speaking soldiers were settled around Addo, 30 kilometres downstream. While they all went into citrus farming, even today there is bar banter about passports being required to move between the two communities. A much bigger problem was elephants.

It turned out that the one thing the pachyderms loved even more than the juicy, delicious and super nutritious spekboom (*Portulacaria afra*), one of the key species of valley bushveld, was oranges. You could understand why, given their sweet, juicy abundance in the irrigated fields. And if there's one thing that is even harder to keep out of cultivated fields than baboons, it's elephants.

It wasn't known then that it was not so much the juicy inside of the fruit that they were going mad for, but the white stuff that lies between the bitter rind and the fruit vesicles: the soft, white, seemingly tasteless pith. Elephants have rather inefficient digestive systems, being able to extract only about 20 per cent of the nutrition from their forage.

That pith, though, is packed with Vitamin C, has loads of fibre, and also – and most importantly for the elephants – pectin (the stuff you use to make jellies and jams). The chemical process of digesting pectin ramps up the animals' ability to extract nutrients up to four-fold. Another thing that is four-fold is an elephant's sense of smell compared to that of a bloodhound. If there is citrus anywhere near, or even far, they will go after it like Assyrian wolves on the fold.

And they did around Kirkwood and Addo, what with all those neat, regimented rows of low-hanging fruit, so to say, and no way for the farmers to keep them out other than shooting them on sight. Once citrus was introduced, the humans and elephants of Addo got on like a wild bush fire, in the worst way.

There is no good data about how many elephants lived in the Addo bush at that time, but no matter how many it was far too many for the local farmers whose lives and crops they were ruining. The authorities were duly petitioned, and in 1919 the administrator of the Cape Province agreed: a brave hunter was needed to go in there and sort them out, once and for all.

All other hunters declined the call, but come the time come Major P.J. Pretorius, hero of the East Africa Campaign against German General von Lettow-Vorbeck's forces. For the task he had made a special, full-length leather hunting coat in order to penetrate the dense bush as unscathed as could be. Pretorius had been a fine soldier and he made a very fine elephant hunter. In just one year he reckons he shot 120, although other sources claim it was a paltry 90.

Whichever, eventually the slaughter sickened him and he in turn petitioned the same administrator to save the last few, maybe only 16, possibly 12, or even fewer. After years of wrangling and red tape, an elephant reserve was proclaimed on a relatively small 2 000-hectare piece of land, in 1931. But the problem of how to let his charges know the new rules had first warden Trollope in a fix. By around 1950 the elephants' rate of reproduction was only just keeping abreast of the rate at which neighbouring farmers were killing them.

The solution came with the erection of the first known elephant-proof fence, made with railway sleepers and cables from old gold mine headgears. In time some of the bigger bulls did learn how to break out, but with various expansions over the years (Zuurberg and Woody Cape being notable) Addo is finally on its way to becoming one of South Africa's mega national parks.

When large-mammal scientist Anthony Hall-Martin was posted to Addo as a postdoctoral researcher, he was given the job of collecting data on what were known to be the most irate pachyderms in Africa. He spent his first few years there just trying to get close to them and being repeatedly charged: including one full-on charge by a herd numbering in excess of 20 animals that had him racing for his life. Then one day he decided to call their bluff (some time previously he had experienced a mock charge in Malawi's Liwonde National Park) when he was rushed by the matriarch Patsy and her herd of nine.

First, he did the usual, which was to zoom off in his Landy, as they expected, but for only a short distance before coming to a halt. The elephants charged again, but then stopped in a cloud of dust just one vehicle length away. They trumpeted at him, stripped and threw branches, bellowed … then didn't seem to know what to do. They quietened down, started shuffling around as though embarrassed. One started to feed, then another, and they slowly moved off. He repeated this with the other herds until they started to ignore him. Finally, his serious work could begin.

By the time he married a few years later, he and his wife, and later their two daughters, could move around Africa's most feared elephants with ease, but still with caution. "We loved those animals, and they came to tolerate us," he once told me, with modesty, and also a large chunk of understatement.[7]

The elephants of Addo (several hundred currently), once murderous at the mere sight of a human, have become among the most docile on the continent. Elephants are like that: they remember things.

ON ANY GIVEN DAY YOU can hear the multitude of tour guides on top of Table Mountain or at Cape Point telling phalanxes of tourists that the furry little critters they're ogling – the rock hyrax (*Procarvia capensis*) – are the African elephant's closest living relative. It's not so much that it is a complete porky pie, but rather that it gives a false impression that they are tight, genetically speaking.

---

[7] You can read the story of the baby elephant and the human baby in the second book in the Stories from the Veld series, *The Game Ranger, the Knife, the Lion and the Sheep: 20 Tales about Curious Characters from Southern Africa*, chapter 2, "Addo Babies".

Of course, the closet living relative to an African (savanna we assume) elephant is an African forest elephant, after that an Asian elephant and, going back millions of years, they were all three closely related to all manner of extinct mammoths and other Eliphantidae. In fact, between the Asian and African species there lies a morass of various extinct elephantine lineages.

On the tree of life, the animals that all elephants are most closely related to are called Sirenias (sea cows), which comprises two distinct groups: the Dugonidae and the Trichechidae. The former being dugongs with only one surviving species, and the latter manatees with three. They, together with the three extant species of elephants, are indeed distant cousins of the hyraxes.

If one wants to be good at one's job, one really needs to dig a little deeper than the tour guide course notes, or modern safari myth. Did you know, for example, that rock hyraxes kill more people in Africa than any other member of Paenungulata,[8] other than elephants and dugongs (we don't get manatees around here)?

OF ALL THE ANIMALS OF Africa, few have been more persecuted by humans than the almost-hooved ones. Dugongs occur in the tropics of the Indian Ocean and southwest Pacific. Their distribution is now highly fragmented and many populations are close to extinct, or have already disappeared. Along the East African coast, into the 1970s, herds of up to 500 animals were not uncommon. Today it is thought there are fewer than 50 – in total.

You might think hyraxes would have escaped the human onslaught, and that is mostly true in Southern Africa. However, in the East African highlands where they are a sought-after delicacy (dassie on a stick) they have been hunted to extinction in some areas, notably the Rwenzori Mountains. Elephants of course we know much more about: in fact, they've been studied and probed in just about every conceivable way, and there's not much we don't know about them from tail to teeth.

Looking inside your gift elephant's mouth you'll notice it has only

---

[8] The clade of "sub-ungulates" (mammals with "almost" hooves), including all three groups mentioned and all of their extinct ancestors.

premolar and molar chewing teeth. Unlike humans who first develop milk teeth, to be replaced by adult teeth, elephants have only the latter. There are six sets top and bottom, which grow from the back of the jaw and move forward, successively pushing out the front ones. They are left with their last pair at around age 40, which have to last for the rest of their lives. Which is why, under natural conditions, they usually die of slow starvation.

They do have one other kind of tooth, their tusks, which are modified incisor teeth. In this case they do start with a pair of milk tusks that are replaced by adult ones within their first year. While both sexes of the savanna species usually have tusks, those of males are typically much thicker and therefore heavier (about a third of the mass is nerve).

Once upon a time tusks weighing 90 kilograms or more were quite commonly seen; today 40 kilograms would be considered a trophy specimen (heaven forbid). Killing for ivory over millennia has gradually reduced the gene pool for big tuskers, causing a "natural" selection for smaller tusks and also tusklessness in some populations. Of course, elephants are not the only animals that carry ivory, also hippos, walruses and narwhals, each of which has been targeted at various times.

Mammoths had by far the biggest tusks ever known and the trade in mammoth tusks is a recent boom industry. As permafrost melts in the Arctic region, large hauls of mammoth ivory are being uncovered. This includes the dwellings of former peoples who built their entire homes with them. Should you want to research the rumoured existence of elephant graveyards you'd want to start digging in the permafrost: large caches have been dislodged where steep muddy hillsides or riverbanks have collapsed.

There are records going as far back as 500 years BCE (before current epoch) of ivory being traded to the Middle East and later Europe. Because of their size and weight, the ivory and slave trades grew in a kind of antibiosis relationship (the opposite of a mutually beneficial – symbiotic – one). Old illustrations of slave caravans invariably show the forlorn, shackled wretches carrying tusks towards coastal ports.

The advent of firearms greatly escalated the ivory trade: far easier to shoot a rampaging bull elephant with a gun than try to spear it. However, for the first six or seven decades into the 20th century, demand for ivory products (mainly piano keys, billiard balls and ornaments in the Western sphere) dissipated due to hard times, along with the invention of plastic replacements. Then the re-emergence of Japan as an economic player in the 1970s drove up demand again. It was used primarily for hankos, or traditional name seals, which previously had been made mainly from wood. From there the craving for ivory and the profits it could realise rolled across much of eastern Asia.

The largest centre for working ivory was for some time Hong Kong. But it now has to compete with places like Laos and Vietnam, which rival the old port nation-city in the production of cheap curios. Most of the ivory workshops are located deep in jungles in order to evade the law; Chinese tourists are bused in to these factories to buy ivory knick-knacks, along with rhino horn and pangolin scales.

About 75 000 African elephants are being killed each year to supply these jungle workhouses. There is a belief in parts of Asia where people have never seen a real elephant that the trade is okay because tusks are shed each year, like deer antlers. No doubt the dealers like to keep that myth alive and not show images of slaughtered animals.

Part of the blame must fall on us, though, the African countries that are bickering over the right to trade versus blanket conservation. Because of the resultant grey areas, CITES (the Convention on International Trade in Endangered Species: note "trade") has rubber stamped sales from member countries and bestowed on China – now the biggest consumer – "approved buyer" status. It's a mess and a tragedy.

IT'S HARD TO IGNORE AN elephant, especially when it's in the room, or is bearing down on you. If you've ever been charged by an ear-flapping, trumpeting behemoth and survived, you'll know just how enervating it is. Even if you haven't, you've probably seen video clips of cars being rolled, or sat upon, by either an enraged bull in musth, or possibly one that is simply bored, or fed up with pesky tourists. Ear flapping and trunk up, for the record, is a good thing since it signals a mock charge just to show you you've annoyed it. Ears laid flat and trunk rolled under is a problem, because then it's closing in for a kill.

I have had the pleasure a number of times, most notably once while riding my bicycle in Mashatu Private Game Reserve, a wedge of Botswanan wild real estate on the Limpopo River. One minute I was tripping alongside a breeding herd feeding calmly in the mopane bush, the next I was being chased by a furious matriarch and hard tailing it down a gravel road for all I was worth. A bit of data for the books: a mature African elephant can run *at least* 35 kilometres per hour. That's what my bike's computer read and I was only just keeping out of her trunk's reach.

I'm guessing the bunch of noisy riders coming up behind me, who knows, spooked her. One thing we do know is, now that the Addo herd has totally chilled out, those in Mashatu are reputed to be the tetchiest these days. I'm guessing it's because they are still getting blasted at by farmers on either side of the game reserve, for sport as much as to protect crops.

There's a tired old safari joke about how you eat an elephant: one piece at a time. Once the groaning subsides, let's just stop and consider some of those parts, starting with those huge hear-all ears. Herds of elephants walking line astern across the wide savanna seas have been likened to armadas of grey galleons, ears flapping like animal punkah-wallahs.[9]

They do this of course for cooling. Their ears are crisscrossed by a network of fine capillaries that carry warm blood into those biological radiators, where it is flapped about, cooled and returned to the main body some degrees lower. Elephants lack sweat glands so the temperature-control function of those ear flaps (pinnae) is vital for them, especially populations living in arid regions. If ever you've spent time outdoors in fluctuating temperatures, you might have learned how to manage fine temperature control by covering or uncovering your ears.

Far more complex in design is the trunk, a veritable biological

---

[9] The word "punkah" derives from the Hindi-word "punkhû," referring to the wings of birds that cause a draft when flapped. A "wallah" is a person engaged in some form of work, such as a rickshaw-wallah or fan-waving punkah-wallah.

marvel. In the early stages of embryonic development the upper lip and nose are separate. However, some time before birth they fuse into that very distinctive proboscis that, more than any other part, defines the animals. Some of its functions include breathing (of course, its primary job), smelling, touching and feeling, grasping, and the production of sound through nature's longest wind instrument.

In technical lingo this elongated appendage is called a muscular hydrostatic – a body part made of muscle but with no supporting skeletal structure, same as our tongues. A big difference, though, is that while our tongues are operated by just eight muscles, an elephant's trunk has an astonishing 150 000 give or take. Your entire body has a paltry 639.

They are bundled in muscle fascicles or paired muscle groups and, as you can imagine, how they work is quite intricate. The outer or superficial ones are divided into dorsal (back), ventral (front) and lateral (side), while the inner sets contain transverse (axial) and radial (different fibres having varying lines of action). Now imagine all those working together to, say, pick up a peanut, peel an orange or pluck some tasty herb from the grassland. African elephants alone have one special feature at their trunk tips: two projections, called fingers, that allow them to wipe an eye or lift a small car, break open a nutshell without cracking the nut inside or give your car a roll if you get too close.

But, while our eyes are titillated by flapping ears and trumpeting trunks, we easily overlook the elephant's equally remarkable feet. To begin, those of our familiar savanna species have five toes on each foot, but only four nails (sub-hooves) on each of the front, and three on the back feet (African forest elephants have five fore and four aft, which was one reason they were split off into a new species).

It is stupefying seeing elephants walking across the veld making absolutely no noise – other than sometimes a low-frequency rumbling they emit when making contact with others out of view. I always thought it was their stomachs rumbling, given what abundantly flatulent animals they are.

Since they spend most of their long lives walking great distances, those feet need to be kept in tip-top shape. Basically, they stand,

and move, on the tips of their fingers and toes, cushioned by thick subcutaneous pads. Think of "memory foam" outdoor seat cushions. To help absorb the impact of a mechanical force delivered by up to eight tonnes, their toes gain extra support from a unique set of cartilaginous rods called the prepollex or prehallux.

If ever you've seen a jumbo seeming to be chilling out, leaning on its front legs, it is a very specific kind of behaviour called "freezing": they are listening intently. Elephants are known to communicate through seismic vibrations, sent out by feet hitting the ground, or received through their feet and sent up the front legs to the middle ear. Inside those foot cushions are cartilaginous nodes similar in function to "acoustic fat" in whales. The ground vibrations of an elephant charging can send a seismic alarm signal for a considerable distance, tens of kilometres away. When vocalising they can communicate up to about 15 kilometres.

In the wild, elephants exercise those multifaceted feet by digging, walking over uneven ground and rubbing their fat pads against objects to keep them lubricated and supple, and the nails and heels trimmed. (Remember when they used to be sold in furniture shops as ashtray stands or ottomans?)

In captivity, however, they live mostly on concrete floors, often covered in faeces and urine, straw if they are lucky, often with little opportunity for walking around. As a result, the pads become dry and cracked and are prone to diseases. It is thought that half of all elephant deaths in captivity start with poor foot care.

ANYONE WHO HAS WATCHED THEM for an appreciable amount of time knows for sure that elephants have big hearts. The weight of that of the average savanna elephant's heart is around 20 kilograms, compared to ours at an average of 250 grams in women and 280 grams in men. Granted the big pachyderms have much bigger machinery to operate relative to ours, but there's much more to their big hearts than that.

Working together with their highly developed 20-kilogram brains, it is believed by people who study these things that elephants manifest a wide range of behaviours we would normally describe as being human, even spiritual. For example, they show high levels of social cooperation. They play and have been noted mimicking human speech and the sound of trucks. They show compassion and even grief. They use tools, although not in any sophisticated way (such as using branches as fly swatters).

It's believed a significant part of those large brains (the cerebrum and hippocampus) is devoted to memory. Elephant herds will live through numerous cycles of flood and famine, so in order to survive they need to know – to remember – when it's time to hit the road and follow some ancient migratory route to greener pastures.

Anyone whose job has been to keep them enclosed knows all too well how they use large branches to break fences. But they also use smaller ones to clean their ears, or wounds, or to scratch. Even more remarkable is that they have been seen to come to the aid of distressed animals, both their own kind as well as others in trouble, including humans (they remember, remember?).

They also appear to show grief, although not all scientists agree on this and so debate rages as to whether or not they exhibit emotions. In some circles it is taboo to suggest that when they congregate around the body of a deceased animal and pass the bones around, it is out of any kind of sentiment. Just curious interest insists this school.

It was South Africa's foremost elephant researcher, the previously mentioned Dr Anthony Hall-Martin, who observed what surely must stand as some kind of documentation of their anthropomorphic behaviour. While working in Addo Elephant National Park he watched as a herd encircled the body of a recently fallen matriarch and her forlorn calf.

The calf was visibly weeping and vocalising by making screaming sounds, while the rest of the herd was rumbling loudly. They stroked (caressed) the dead female's body and some tried to lift it. Then suddenly, at some point which the person watching could not discern, they all fell silent. Some of the adults began to kick dirt over the body, others to break off tree branches and lay them over her. For two days they stood vigil, occasionally going off to drink but always returning.

I think there is a strong argument in favour of the notion that this was something beyond mere curious interest.

One Loony Bird, a Funny Monkey and the Most Barefaced Botanical Heist in History

If you stand in the veld long enough staring down a tree, by the time you blink its name is likely to have been changed. Remember the one we used to call the apple-ring thorn tree, also the ana tree, *Acacia albida*? Next time we looked it had been renamed *Faidherbia albida* after some West African French colonial.

Next it was the rain or apple-leaf tree which we grew up calling *Lonchocarpus capassa*, but no longer. We looked away and when we looked back it was *Philenoptera violacea*. But nothing blind-sided us quite so much as when our acacias became something else entirely. Two somethings in fact.

It is in the kingdom of flowering plants that most renaming occurs. Throughout the 18th and 19th centuries the shipping routes of the world were virtually awash with collectors and their collections sailing between European (and, as it turns out, Asian) courts and the far-flung parts of the globe in a race to gather ever-larger, grander and rarer displays of exotica. Many of the world's most popular garden plants, including orchids, gladioluses, geraniums and even proteas, were collected this way.

The dainty, pink-flowering nerine lily that is often referred to as the Guernsey lily (*Nerine sarniensis*), because that is where British botanists first saw them, is an interesting case. Given its island location, it was assumed they were an endemic species there. The species name refers to Sarnia, the old Roman name for Guernsey.

There is an unlikely story that bags of seeds from South Africa, where it is in fact endemic, destined for Holland, were tossed from a floundering ship somewhere in the English Channel back in 1659.

The flotsam washed up and took root there, where they are now the virtual national flower, if that island was a sovereign nation (which many people there wish it was). More likely they were taken there by the Right Rev. William Herbert, an expert on the amaryllis family, who both cultivated and named them back in 1820. Where he got them is anyone's guess and, although they did not originate in Guernsey, the name remains.

The faidherbia incident, on the other hand, turned out to be only the first shot fired across the taxonomic bow of things acacia. Probably nothing is as iconically *of* this continent as a vista of wide savanna punctuated by stately acacia thorn trees, canopies unfurled, with maybe a giraffe or two completing the scene. However, these days only a trained botanist would be able to identify those trees as belonging to the new *Vachellia* (such as the flat-crowned *tortillis*) or *Senegalia* groups (like the common hook-thorn *S. caffra* or the black-thorn *S. mellifera*).

Early in the 21st century botanists started thinking that, at the genetic level, the one large group of African acacias was really two quite distinct genera. Apparently around 30 million years ago one of them (Vachellia) had walked eastwards out of the forests of West Africa into the savannas and started a new genetic lineage. Some 10 million years later another (Senegalia) followed, and by then they had diverged into two quite distinct groups.

Both common sense and the rules of taxonomy would lead quite easily to a strategy of keeping one of them in the taxon of acacias and the others in a new genus. Even more compelling would be the fact that the type specimen is (or was) *A. nilotica*, meaning "thorn tree found along the Nile".

Known since antiquity as gum Arabic, or gum sudani, it was first scientifically described and given its Latin name back in 1754. This should have ensured it would forever after be an acacia. But that was not to be, due to the data fiddling and fact fudging of some bast... erm, botanists in Australia.

For the average oke on the platteland this isn't going to mean a leaf or a twig. Your sweet-thorn and his soetdoring are going to remain acacias and hardly anyone will give a hoot. In fact, for the present at least (as though in a fit of guilty concession), even in scientific papers you are allowed to refer to the African species of the kind as acacias.

Tree spotting has never really caught on like bird spotting, so while we have the well-established sub-culture of birding, treeing is not really a thing. Birders also make a lot more noise, twitching and tweeting and twittering away. When they see a rare bird they are given to squawking. They also squawk when some well-known and no doubt loved species is given a new name and, heaven forbid, a new *Roberts* number.

Birders have much in common with British train spotters, otherwise known as anoraks (for their preferred dress code). Both groups are hobbyist collectors, and what they collect primarily is numbers. They don't like it when the number of a beloved steam train is changed through the process of rationalisation. In the case of birds a change in taxonomy will alter its place on the branches of the evolutionary family tree of birds, and that will invariably lead to a new number being assigned in the bird book of books, *Roberts Birds of Southern Africa* (simply called *Roberts* by those in the bizz).

Among the first big outbreaks of squawking was back in the mid-1980s when ornithologists, using the latest genetic profiling, discovered that what had long been considered a single group of francolins, was in fact two: the true francolins and the spurfowls. The true francolins were of noble African origin, while the spurfowls were directly descended from the Asian forest fowl, better known to us as the common or farmyard chicken. The two groups were in fact not close enough to call one another family.

The problem for old-time birders was manifold. First was the issue that the two groups all looked alike: so similar that only the serious game-bird experts could tell a red-winged francolin from a red-billed spurfowl, any more than a Cape spurfowl from an Orange River francolin, other than by their respective distributions. It could take a lifetime to see them all, and another to tell them apart. And that's before we start on the bewildering warbler family.

There is a strong movement worldwide, among mostly professional ornithologists, and most specifically those working in Great Britain under the hawk-like watch of such august organisations as the British Ornithologists' Union (BOU, founded 1858), to have the common names for birds standardised worldwide. A case in point is when our barn swallow arrives in Wales where it is welcomed as a common swallow. Or that our familiar green-backed heron might be a mangrove heron in Indonesia, or a striated one elsewhere.

If your job is to study birds, especially migratory ones, it makes sense to have your subject known by the same (English at least) name from Svalbard to Saldahna Bay. Likewise, one can understand the move to rename the African robins since our robin-chats bear only scant resemblance to little European robin red-breasts of snow-bedecked Christmas cards. But not everyone likes to have to call a Knysna lourie a turaco, or a dikkop a thick-knee. They're ours, we can call them whatever we chose.

Our plovers, or some of them, are another case in point. We used to lump a large group of birds under the mantle of plover, much as we once did with acacia trees. But the reality is that some of our plovers are not true plovers at all. The larger, mainly inland varieties are really lapwings, while generally speaking the plovers are those little, mostly white birds that run up and down on beaches or along the shores of coastal lagoons.

Quite a few of the birds found in Southern Africa are also resident in, or migratory to, East Africa. That dispute could have gone either way, but given the general disdain among postcolonials there for us boertjies ever since we gave their empress a bloody nose, the jolly old chaps of the BOU tend to side with their birding chums in East Africa when it comes to standardising the common names of our shared species. Which is why where we used to have a dikkop, or in fact two (spotted and water), we now have thick-knees.

As with the acacias, the Southern African warblers of old were really always too diverse to have been lumped into one group. The first edition of *Roberts* (1940) names 59 warbler species, whereas the latest has just 31. The others have been split into the groups apalis, camaroptera, cisticola, eremomela and prinia. When it comes to giving things their most proper scientific names, I am all for the new ways.

However, when it comes to common names, I often find myself leaning with the old guard. Take an old feathered acquaintance of mine, the one we used to know as the bleating bush warbler but is now the green-backed camaroptera (the charming Afrikaans bostingtinkie better describes its voice).

Why shouldn't we keep on calling it a bush warbler even though its new Latin name is *Camaroptera brachyura*? Forgive me if sometimes I get carried away with the minutiae of these things, but that's only because *they* started it! Names are coined in order to make things easy, and there is no way that a green-backed camaroptera is any easier than a bleating bush warbler to identify or enjoy.

The first name given to our green-backed camaroptera was *Sylvia brachyura*, the short-tailed sylvia. This was bestowed by the French ornithologist Louis Jean Pierre Vieillot, who named it from a stuffed specimen collected here by the naturalist-explorer François le Vaillant. Given how the warblers have been sliced up again and then again, it's hardly surprising his "sylvia" has not survived.

THE STORY OF FRANÇOIS LE Vaillant[10] and his travels in South Africa is among the most beguiling of the time, namely 1781–1784. At that time the Cape of Good Hope was a much-favoured hunting ground for collectors as well as hunters: most often the two were one and the same. And I use the word "beguiling" in most of its senses, as we'll see: I might as well have said begulling.

Back in the 1700s just about the only point of entry for most Europeans into Africa was South Africa, specifically the Cape of Good Hope. However, it still wasn't easy. The Dutch East India Company kept the door to Table Bay under a tight lock and unless you knew someone high up who could introduce you to the governor, or you had been conscripted to work there, your passage beyond the bay would be barred.

---

[10] He actually usually spelled his name Levaillant, but on the wall of the Heerenlogement he engraved it simply as F. Vailant. See Stories from the Veld vol. III, *Of Hominins, Hunter-Gatherers and Heroes: 20 Amazing Places in South Africa*, chapter 18.

As it happened François was very well connected. His mother was a foster sister to King Louis XVI no less (by dint of her mother having been the future king's one-time wet nurse). Perhaps equally relevant is the fact that his father, Etienne, had worked for the Dutch West India Company, or that the governor of the colony of Suriname at the time, one Johan Raye van Breukelerwaard, was the recipient of part of Francois's famous bird collection on his return from Africa. That kind of patronage has always opened otherwise locked doors.

Maybe it was Le Vaillant's stifling marriage back home, with two young children (he writes rather poorly of them in his travel memoirs), that caused him to virtually hit the shore at Table Bay running. First the Frenchman spent some considerable time exploring and collecting in the southwestern Cape. However, when he watched from the shore as his entire collection until that time blew up with the ship on which it was stowed in Saldahna Bay, it seems to be a catalyst that spurred him onwards.

The first of his two big journeys was eastwards to the edge of the colonial boundary. He was not the first paleface to venture that far, as the route had already been trodden by hunters and the Trek Boer vanguard, as well as the likes of Swedish botanist-explorer Anders Sparrman and even Governor Baron Joachim von Plettenberg. Nevertheless, the territory as a whole was still largely uncharted and Le Vaillant breathed in the untamed expanses.

On this odyssey he was accompanied by five servants, foremost among whom was his handlanger, or major-domo, Klaas, who seems to have become a close companion and of whom he wrote with some affection (certainly more so than of his own family). Of Klaas's wife Rachel, we learn almost nothing, excepting for the colour illustration of her in his published "travels". Klaas, on the other hand, had a bird named after him, one of the three small green cuckoos of the subcontinent. That was about as high praise as could be conferred.

The explorer's description of the bird is a virtual eulogy to his camp companion, which is curious since elsewhere the Khoi man is described as being "sly and redoubtable". The second adjective could mean duplicitous, or exceptionally strong, alarming or funny, but in a funny peculiar way. Since that author's source could have been only Le Vaillant's own writings, it might be that the Frenchman was pulling one of his many literary jests.

In Afrikaans the name of Klaas's cuckoo is "meitjie" from its call *mei-tjie, mei-tjie* (may-kie, meaning "maiden"), which can go on incessantly for 20 minutes at a time. It might be that Klaas was something of a Rosinante, the name Cervantes gave to Don Quixote's horse. In Spanish the name means old horse, or old nag, so one who might complain at length. Yet Klaas still has his bird while there is not a Rachel's anything in our index of natural things.

Le Vaillant was taken with not only the big game, but the insects, the plants and all the varying groups of people he met, and he illustrated most of them. However, most of all he was captivated by the birds (and, if you'll permit the slight, one bird in particular). Of note is the strange fact that, for reasons not known, in all his travels he noted only one water bird, the greater flamingo, and none of the numerous thick-billed seed-eating species he would have seen.

Nevertheless he is considered to be our first proper ornithologist and bird illustrator. When back home he commissioned a number of leading artists to help him produce 300 colour copper-plate reproductions depicting 284 bird species for his two-volume *Traveller in Africa* (*Voyage dans l'intérieur de l'Afrique*), as well as the later *Natural History of African Birds* (*Histoire naturelle des oiseaux d'Afrique*). That's something like having commissioned Pierneef to do the woodcuts for your own travelogue.

Among those plates is a trogon, which some people consider to be the most attractive, if extremely shy, of all our splendiferous avian assemblage. There is also a colour plate of a Khoi maiden named Narina among the Gonaqua people he met. Somewhere along the Great Fish River, it is believed near Somerset East, he spent time at the spacious homestead of a Khoi headman, a place he calls Kok's Kraal.

There lived the Khoi teenager named Narina, apparently meaning "flower" in her now-extinct Gonaqua language. It appears the Frenchman was smitten, but was in turn spurned, by her (or possibly by her mother). At one time he resorted to spying on her while she swam with her friends in a pool of the Great Fish River. When he appropriated their leather aprons and then taunted them, Narina's mother came to rescue their dignities. Remember, this was a middle-aged man with a wife and children back home.

It is likely that he first noted and then named the fetching bird we know as the Narina trogon in the glade surrounded by dense forest at a place called Pampoenkraal: a level spur of land wedged between the deep chasms of the Swart and Kaaimans rivers. He outspanned there on both the outward and return legs of his journey, a place now known as the Saasveld forestry college (which has been incorporated as a satellite campus of Nelson Mandela University). He noted it was the most attractive bird he saw in all his wonderings.

With Le Vaillant it is difficult to separate the real from the fanciful, and he was a great romantic. When it was time to present himself at Kok's Kraal he spent an entire morning dressing in most extravagant attire (which he describes with relish).

The first thing you might notice about his travelogue is that the title alludes to Africa, whereas in fact he travelled no further than the Great Fish River eastwards, and the Orange River northwards. Then there are the illustrations. He includes a number of animals – for example a South American jaguar and an Asian elephant – clearly not found in Africa at all.

Unquestionably he was a dedicated naturalist and a talented artist. But evidence suggests he was also a bit of a loony bird. When it came to the avifauna, he also included species not found in Africa. But he went even further out on a fanciful limb: he illustrated at least ten birds that are unrecognisable, and another ten that are obviously completely concocted. And yet, later, he complained bitterly about not being taken more seriously as a scientist.

There is no clear answer as to what prompted these flights of fantasy. My guess is that, much like another great South African bird illustrator Claude Gibney Finch-Davies,[11] he suffered from the madness of a true collector. In the case of Le Vaillant it might have been the result of seeing so much of his collection, along with all his instruments, blown sky high, and much of the rest having been

---

[11] See Stories from the Veld II, *The Game Ranger, the Knife, the Lion and the the Sheep: 20 Curious Characters from Southern Africa*, chapter 5, "The Artist Who Flew Too Close to the Sun".

promised to various patrons and collectors back in Europe. But that's just my guesswork.

While paging through Le Vaillant's colour plates one is challenged even further. Most of his illustrations are accurate and most quite superb, particularly those of his flower collection. He did watercolours while specimens were still fresh in order to capture their true beauty, before being pressed, shipped back to France and handed over to professional illustrators to render for his books. But some are truly awful, like the "black monkey" (Plate 111), which is clearly meant to be a baboon.

What is most odd about it is that he had a pet baboon named Kees that would, when tired, ride on the back of one of his dogs. He did an anatomically correct painting of Kees (Plate 78), so why the discrepancy? I suspect it is another fictitious creature.

Whichever way you judge him his name persists, not only literally carved in stone at the Heerenlogement cave up in Namaqualand, but in the birds he named: Klaas's cuckoo, Narina trogon, gabar goshawk, malachite sunbird (*Le sucrier malachitte*), trac-trac chat (*Le tractrac*), the fish eagle "vocifer" and the bateleur, acrobat in French, the rocking, gliding flight of which reminded him of the movements of a tight-rope walker.

Then there are those that were named in honour of the man himself who is considered the originator of South African ornithology: the crested barbet (*Trachyphonus vaillantii*), Levaillant's cisticola, the now-endangered Cape parrot, the red-winged francolin, southern tchagra, as well as his very own cuckoo (the striped one).

A last anecdote on the naming of birds involves an eagle and an eagle owl, which has nothing to do with Le Vaillant, but another French connection. One is the bird we used to know as the black eagle and now Verreauxs' eagle, and the other the giant eagle owl, but now called the Verreaux's eagle owl. The astute among readers will have noticed the difference in placement of that tricky little apostrophe.

Early editions of *Roberts* got it right, but since then just about all bird book editors have assumed that one must have been an error and so made them both "Verreaux's" (one notable exception being the unexpurgated *Roberts Birds of Southern Africa, VIIth Edition*, scientific editors Hockey, Dean and Ryan). Someone in the team knew their birds as well as their history and grammar.

The story of the eagle and the eagle owl starts with the Verreaux family of French naturalists and taxidermists, who ran the most successful taxidermy business in Paris during the early to mid-19th century, Maison Verreaux. The maison funded collecting expeditions all over the world and, at one stage, fils Jules was sent out to collect fresh specimens in South Africa. While out here, in 1825, he assisted the naturalist-explorer Andrew Smith to found the South African Museum of Natural History in Cape Town.

As could be expected, Jules collected many things exotic and strange, including the body of a recently buried Tswana warrior which he exhumed, preserved and sent back to Paris to "show". Among his collections was a large milky coloured owl as well as a black eagle.

The finding of the owl was credited to him alone. But the eagle must have been collected later when he had been joined by frère Edouard, and possibly even after that when oncle Pierre Antoine had joined them in Africa. So it was that Verreaux's eagle owl was named for Jules alone, while Verreauxs' eagle for Jules et Edouard, and possibly also Uncle Pierre, but we'll never know for sure.

One quick last note here on "collecting". What it really means is shooting, usually with a shotgun, in order to observe, describe and finally preserve the specimen. I was once told by the director of the Natural History Museum of Zimbabwe in Bulawayo how one overzealous collector had completely annihilated a local population of the African broadbill near Victoria Falls.

François le Vaillant devised a smart method of shooting birds without overly disfiguring their plumage: he would charge his shotgun with gunpowder, seal it with a candle stub, then pour water down the barrel. This he held upwards while preparing to discharge at his subject. If the water dispatched it, it would remain intact, but if the candle-end delivered the coup de grace one can imagine feathers flying.

WE CAN APPRECIATE AND EVEN welcome how modern research has found new relationships between organisms where before we did not see them or, more frequently, shown that there was none where we thought there had been. The African acacias being a case in point.

It turned out that the bas… pardon me, botanists in the land of Oz had been extremely busy making arrangements for the International Botanical Congress that was to be held in Melbourne in 2005. One thing they did was to compile a long list of reasons why the African acacias should be not only split, but also renamed and none of them as an actual acacia. That name should be bestowed upon their own group of Australian trees which they call wattles (the same ones that invade our mountains, coastal dune fields and riverbanks).

When it came time to a show of hands, what with the benches loaded with wattle-friendly voters, the IBC acceded and handed the genus name "acacia" to Australia – a country that did not even exist when the first African acacia was scientifically described, thereby breaking all known rules of taxonomy. Rumour has it that among those in the Australian camp were South African emigrées eager to prove their new-found allegiance to the land down under.

At the meeting in 2005 the local cabal even had a new type specimen waiting in a ribbon-wrapped box to present to the XVIII IBC meeting – *A. penninervis*, the common old mountain hickory wattle. And therein lies the final affront: Australians don't even call theirs "acacias". Even the national tree of Australia is called the golden wattle, *A. pycnantha*.

If there was any justice in the corridors of the botanical fraternity the golden wattle would have been given the name *Racosperma pycnantha*, while the concocted genus *Vachellia* should have retained the sacred name *Acacia*. First we had to contend with Breaker Morant, then that embarrassing ball tampering episode, and now this!

Unlike the green-backed camaroptera, however, I suspect "acacia" is one name we'll not give up without one final braai showdown.

"We're Okay, We have Fire": Five Go on an Even Bigger Adventure

WE HAD SO MUCH FUN on our first trip to "The Swamps", we decided on a repeat performance as soon as we were sprung from the military. For round two we recruited two more bush-loving old school mates, Neil and Ant. The plan, though, was outwardly much the same: catch a train from Johannesburg to Francistown, from there hitch a ride on a supply truck to Maun, then find our way into the Okavango and see what happened.

Over the intervening year Don had been busy studying his map and noticed the feint markings of an airstrip, the only one, almost dead centre in the Delta. We duly caught our train and then got a lift on top of a pile of very angular boxes on the back of a truck from Francistown to Maun. It must not have been overly exciting because the only thing I recall of that trip were the corners of large boxes sticking into me, no matter which way I turned.

Actually there was one thing: every now and again the old grey-grizzled man who had ordered the truck to stop for us, would yell "Patience!" and then something in Setswana which we could not follow. "Patience!" It went on all trip, maybe 18 hours of it. The old man was a trader from Maun who had been on a shopping trip to Francistown and was ferrying his wares home. Only right at the end did we work out Patience was the old man's young handlanger at whom he would regularly bark instructions. For the rest of our trip, "Patience!" became the call to action.

And I nearly forgot, there was another brush with adventure

before we even got on that truck. We'd arrived in Francistown in the evening, decamped on the railway station platform and then walked into town in search of a drink. The first pub we spied we entered – and the place fell ominously silent. We ordered beers and, given the hostile stares, thought it best to beat a hasty retreat with them back to the station. The fact that ours were the only white faces in the place did not ring any warning bells: after all we were in Botswana, not racist South Africa.

Back at the station we became aware of a posse out on the hunt. We stuffed our bags through a window and then ourselves into a locked waiting room, then reversed the procedure through a narrow, high window out back. As the last of us was vaselining himself out of the clerestory vent, we were given a jolt of haste by banging on the door.

Making our way very quietly into the surrounding Kalahari thornveld we did our best to imitate "seldom seen" pangolins and, lucky for us, it worked. On the downside it was July and even colder than our previous year's foray into the wilderness. We thought it best not to get snug and warm in our (SA-army issue) sleeping bags, lest we needed to gap it in the night. Consequently we froze our brass-monkey's balls right off.

What we had not considered was the sight of five young white men dressed in an assortment of civvies and military issue bush gear (very good on safari) and that there was a hot bush war going on just over the border. Someone later explained to us that Francistown was a staging post for ZAPU – Zimbabwe African People's Union – "terrorist" raids into then Rhodesia, and we must have looked like nothing so much as a bunch of badly disguised white-regime special ops agents. Talk about falling into a crocodile's lair.

Maun hadn't changed much in a year, excepting when we reached Tony Graham's island haunt we found a fully functioning safari base camp, a fridge full of cold beers and a kitchen that turned out hot goodies. After a bit of R&R at Tony's, we found our way to Maun International – still just a "radio shack" control room and a gravel strip. There we found a young, blond, tanned bush pilot in regulation dress: Raybans, short-sleeve shirt, short rugby shorts and velskoens sans socks.

"We're Okay, We have Fire": Five Go on an Even Bigger Adventure

Don unfurled his treasured map on the gravel and indicated the lone landing strip.

"Ah," nodded our new hope. "Xaxaba, that's the Wilmot's old place. But I don't think anyone operates it anymore."

Nevertheless, R100 (this was a time before the Botswana Pula) would buy us a round trip. We instructed our pilot to drop us off there and fetch us two weeks hence. Hands were shaken. We piled our kit into the single-engined, six-seater Cessna – although it could just as well have been a Piper or a Beechcraft for all I recall – and clambered aboard: destination uncertain.[12]

We flew for maybe an hour, low enough to be able to clearly see elephants around island fringes, hippos bobbing in pools, crocodiles on sand bars, formations of birds flying beneath us, their shadows following across the ground or the surface of the tannin-stained water. It was high-water time in the Delta and everything was swollen, fat, gorged. The ashen X-ray outlines of burnt trees could be seen on the interior of islands where they had fallen when wild fires had torn across the area during the previous dry, brittle, bleak season. It was bewitching to see this sea of land, land of water, a blue-green lens that curved across the horizon.

Our pilot seemed to drop the plane vertically into a clearing surrounded by big trees, then skidded to a halt on a sphincter-clenchingly short dirt runway. It later became apparent that all but the largest islands in the Okavango wetland have a fringe of tall riparian trees – wild figs, mangosteens, waterberries, jackalberries, sometimes a raintree or knobthorn – and a centre devoid of all but the toughest grasses. The islands act as water siphons and left behind are extremely saline interiors. You don't dare try to walk across them barefoot as the short grass stems, usually cropped by semi-aquatic antelope, are like shards of glass.

Our pilot left without further ado as we sat on our packs poring

---

[12] On his gravestone in the Bonaventure cemetery, otherwise made famous as the "garden of good and evil", local Savannah, GA, author Conrad Aiken has chiselled in a fine Gothic font: *Cosmos Mariner – Destination Unknown*. *If you want to find out the full story, and it's a very fine one, you'll just have to read the book by John Berendt.*

over Don's map, trying to interrogate a plan from its cartographic reticence. Talk, dammit! Patience! Then we heard an engine racing towards us and out of the tree line shot a rattling old Series 2 Land Rover driven by a tall, sunburned man with a bokkie bard and wearing the customary safari khakis and veldskoens.

He jumped out and introduced himself as PJ. But what the hell were we doing there, he demanded, a bit nonplussed. All bright eyed and shiny toothed, we explained we were five lads in pursuit of a jolly big adventure.

"Well, I'm afraid you can't do it here."

Our crests drooped.

"We have just started running photo safaris from here and are expecting our first guests to fly in tomorrow. From the USA."

Our crests fell.

"But come on, jump in. I'll take you guys back to camp and we'll make a plan."

Our crests plumped up.

The camp was called Xaxaba as per our map, the old forward hunting base of Wilmot patriarch, the late great Bobby, now being run by the next generation. It was lunchtime and we gladly tucked into the fresh food, oven-warm bread and even beers free of charge. Stuff will happen when you don't expect it.

The plan was that PJ would run us up the Boro channel in his banana boat, to a place he called Biggs's Island. It had lately been the base of an American researcher. Biggs had abandoned the place a few years before ("too many lions"). We could hole up there for two weeks, when our host would return and deliver us to the airstrip for the rendezvous with our pilot.

PJ dropped us off and we were charmed. Overhead was the usual canopy of large riverine trees, with enough fallen branches to give us fire for our duration. Mr Biggs had also bequeathed us several spent oil drums and a roll of fence wire that was soon configured as a raft (by then we were a little wiser to the dangers of swimming with crocodiles), and a water flushed long-drop: the water flowed naturally through the hole and was then filtered in the sandy substrate.

We soon discovered our island was not very large, maybe several hundred metres across, and so a bit of a disappointment when compared with our previous jaunt on Chitabe Island, which was several kilometres end to end. This limited range led to five curious young men looking into the distance and wandering what daily wonders the islands yonder might hold.

The nights were often tense, full of things that go creak and groan, grunt and growl and howl. When you are not very knowledgeable about these things, it's almost impossible to distinguish a tinkling tree frog from the *whee-yooo, whee-yooo* of a thick-knee, or the staccato bark of a bushbuck. Owls are pretty easy, excepting when it's a Pel's fishing-owl whose call sound like, according to the early edition of *Roberts* bird guide I was lugging, lost souls falling into hell. Or a greater galago (bushbaby), that sounds like a baby being given a truly horrendous beating. It tends to keep sleep at arm's length.

One night all hell broke loose overhead, shrieking and barking and crying and moaning that went on for an unbearable time: it was all too human sounding. In the morning we checked the campsite and found it strewn with bloody bits of fur and flesh, all of it a light grey-blue. Clearly a troop of vervet monkeys had swung right into a nest of sleeping baboons, setting off the battle that had raged in the canopy. From the evidence we deduced the monkeys had been given a real beating.

Another night we were besieged by an encirclement of grunts and growls and movement always just beyond the useful reach of our lights. Lions, there was absolutely no doubt, but we couldn't tell how many. We lay down in star formation around the fire, heads in and feet out, with our backpacks and pieces of firewood forming a makeshift kraal. We knew they'd be absolutely useless if the predators decided to attack, but you have to do something.

What you really do is calculate your own odds: one in five, not so bad. It was not the night, of all in his life to date I'm pretty sure, that Neil would have chosen to get gyppo guts, but fate deals you the hand it does. It took a heap of courage on both our counts for him to execute a bush kak, more of a bush splatter, under guard, but I was generously rewarded when we made it out alive later back at Island Safari Lodge.

One day Jerry and I decided to fish from the raft in our private lagoon while Don, Neil and Ant went walkabout. I still have a black-and-white photo of them setting out, already chest deep in reeds, one of them shouldering a panga while under one of their hats lurked the box of matches that would prove a life saver later. What follows is cobbled from reconstructed and deconstructed analyses of events over the years, and it's the best intel I have....

WHEN THE SUN HUNG LOW and the others had not returned, Jerry and I became uneasy. Three youngsters armed with only a panga, wading across islands and river channels and expanses of reed and papyrus beds, in one of Africa's most remote and wildest places – what could possibly go wrong? When darkness began to envelop our camp we realised we might never see them again. Crocodile (most likely possibility), snake (possible), lions (unlikely but not impossible), leopards (much less likely), elephants, hippos, buffaloes, just about anything out there was a contender.

Jerry and I did what we could, which was to make as big a bonfire as we could from ilala palm fronds, in the event that our mates were out there somewhere in the darkness hoping for a shooting star to give them a bearing. For a long time we walked around our own island and called into the night. At one point we thought we heard replies, but from entirely the wrong direction, so we passed it off as a delusion. When there were no more fronds to burn, we had to call it a night and just hope for the best.

The mornings were really chilly, so Jerry and I lay in. We both had not slept well and, anyway, we had no idea what we might do next. Setting off to look for three people in a wetland larger than Denmark, with only an unreliable hint of a direction, was fraught with complications. We were flicking sticks into the fire when the sound of a distant boat engine roused us. We rushed over to the lediba and then jumped for joy when a motorboat chugged into our lagoon ferrying our lost boys.

Without a care for formalities or lurking danger, the three jumped into the shallows and shouted farewells to their rescuers. It transpired Don did in fact have a compass. However, they'd spent their time

"We're Okay, We have Fire": Five Go on an Even Bigger Adventure

zigging and zagging to look at things here and there and, when it came time to turn for home, realised three things: they had only the vaguest idea of their back direction, they had little idea what distance they'd covered, and they were confronted by a chimera of reed beds and tree lines all looking very much the same. Imagine you are in a dense forest and only one gap in the trees will lead you to safety, but every gap looks the same. Which one do you take, Hansel?

In the event they had all but made it, having walked right over our home island and kept on going until darkness overtook them. That accounted for us hearing them calling from what we thought was the wrong direction. Eventually they too had to call it a day, so decided to make camp. With their matches they made a fire and stripped off their clothes, which they hung on surrounding branches.

That was when they heard us calling. Backlit by dancing flames, they called back: "We have fire. We are okay." This calling back and forth must have gone on for about an hour, which was when they heard a motorboat approaching. The three thought they were saved. Another half hour passed with much to'ing and fro'ing on the part of the boat, and much shouting between the landward and the swampward parties. Eventually the boat managed to get within about 50 metres of the stranded lads, only to say they would be back in the morning. The three lost lads were downcast. But hey, they had fire.

Duly the next morning the rescue was enacted and by 08h00 our mates were dropped off at our camp on Biggs's Island. It turned out that, in a place with few named landmarks, ours turned out to be a life saver. Donald was not spared any scorn over his navigational skills.

Many years later I befriended a barefoot, Bohemian-styled fellow named Peter Sandenbergh who told me his side of the story. At that time he and his trader father were busy building what was possibly the second non-consumptive (i.e. non-hunting) safari lodge in the Okavango, after Xaxaba, which they named Delta Camp. It was, and still is, on the Boro channel not very far from Biggs's Island (which, incidentally, is still known by that name, although some people now call it Baboon Island after a wildlife documentary made there, named "Swamp Troop").

When they heard shouts wafting down the channel on the breeze, they put down their beers, looked at one another, and thought WTF!? Better jump in the old chugger and go for a look-see. No one should be where someone clearly was. What they saw was three stark naked and arum-lily white youths, dancing around a fire chanting: "We have fire – we're okay."

"We weren't going to pull up there in the middle of the night, prowling lions or no," Pete confessed.

Just imagine: visions of lords of the tsetse flies and sticking Piggy easily come to mind. Would you have landed?

Back at Xaxaba, the guests turned out to be a John and Olivia, John flying his own plane in like it was greased lightning.

"And what do you do, John?" PJ had enquired of the ebullient dark-haired guest who'd arrived with a vivacious, blonde Australian woman.

At least PJ had a good laugh about it after his partner castigated him for his boorishness.

"I hadn't watched a movie for years," he admitted.

Our pilot buzzed the camp at the appointed time so we clambered aboard the creaking Landy and bid farewell to this paradise. Back at Island Safari Lodge we spent the afternoon and the evening with our elbows on the riverside pub counter eating freshly baked meat pies (buffalo) and drinking ice-cold Windhoek Export – mine gratis in lieu of my bravery on the night of the big bush evacuation – while listening to the only tape they had: Don Maclean's album *American Pie*.

The five of us staggered out at some dark hour and fell about on the riverbank without bothering to make any attempt at creating a camp of sorts. The morning sun eventually chased us out of our slumbers and we sought shade back at the bar.

"Did you enjoy your visitor last night?" asked our host.

When we replied with puzzled faces he took us back to our sleeping spot and pointed to the set of large reptilian footprints that circumscribed the area.

"That bugger's been watching us from the opposite bank for some weeks now," Tony informed us. "Must be at least 14 feet. Biggest croc I've ever seen down here for a while. Clearly you lads drank so much you were not to its taste."

Also, some years later, when I was an irregular at the Duck Inn, I happened to meet the pilot who'd flown us in and out of Xaxaba the previous decade.

"I wasn't going to come back for you," he admitted. "I thought there was no chance you'd still be alive. Five clueless blokes in the wildest place in Africa!"

Lucky for us his flying colleagues managed to convince him he had a moral obligation as well as a legal contract with us (we'd paid him in advance).

I often wonder what might have been my path in life had he in fact not returned for us. You just never can tell. Either way, since then I have never travelled without a knife of some kind and a lighter.

Why the Long Neck? Giraffes and the Long and the Short of Adaptive Biology

THE GIRAFFE IS SURELY ONE of the Great Artist's culminating masterpieces of elegance in motion and beauty in form. They seem not to jostle, not to bellow, or to fuss much. They are, as some people might observe, just there: tall, quiet and stately as living haikus.

On the acacia plain
Stands silent zirafa still
Dappled, a living tree

Who does not love a giraffe? Most elegant and graceful of all animals, which seem to harm no other, with those beguiling long eyelashes. Just why this leopard-spotted camel, or camel-horse, as they are variously named, should have acquired such a long neck and legs is open to conjecture, but we do find some clues in the museum archives.

Their closest living relative is the okapi of the Central African rainforests, a kind of giraffe-antelope, although they are not as closely related as you might imagine. The two families began to diverge around 11 million years ago (mya), back when almost all of Africa was covered in dense forest.

Around 10 mya Africa began a long cycle of drying up, which resulted in the forest cover declining. It did not happen all in one go, or indeed in just one direction, but in a series of advances and retreats of climatic and vegetational tides. Around five mya South Africa was still mostly covered by forest but, following the opening up of the

Southern Ocean gap between South America and Antarctica, the change accelerated as Southern Africa cooled.

At that time there were various kinds of giraffids living in the forests (up to 10 genera have been identified), including the giant, short-necked giraffe that we know from fossils at the West Coast Fossil Park near Langebaan. The bones of around 500 individuals of the species *Sivatherium hendeyi* have been uncovered in a relic bed of the Berg River from Pleistocene times.

Sivathere (the group name) had a body significantly larger and more muscular than the average modern giraffe, but with a noticeably shorter neck. It stood about three metres tall at the shoulder and four overall, against our modern giraffes at just short of six metres. Nevertheless, they are thought to have weighed about the same, hitting the scales at around one-and-a-quarter tonnes. This animal was both grazer and browser, judging from its teeth.

The most likely scenario is that, as the forests dwindled, early giraffes moved into the savanna mosaic and took increasingly to browsing on the emerging tall fine-leaved and fire-resistant trees where they had virtually no resource competition. Those with longer necks outcompeted their shorter-necked kin, as the mastermind of environmental biology, Charles Darwin, so ingeniously described.

Talking about that long neck, a wildebeest walks into a bar, sits down and glumly orders a Stroh rum.

The bartender asks: "Why the long face?"

"It's because my best mate Jerry won't come in," answers the melancholy antelope.

"Really!" replies the bartender. "Let me go check."

Outside he finds a giraffe standing, peering over the roof.

"Why the long neck?" asks the publican.

"It's not so much my neck that's the problem," replies the giraffe, "it's my legs. Whenever I bend down to have a drink I feel awfully vulnerable."

If ever you've watched a giraffe approaching a waterhole to drink, you'll have noticed how twitchy it is on account of having to lower itself like a four-legged crane. But it's also those legs that give the animals their remarkable fluidity; as they run they seem to float in flowing slow motion across African seas of waving grass. Their name comes from the Arabic *zirafa*, which you sometimes find translated as "the lovely one" and that would be charming, but it is not true. What it really means "one who walks swiftly".

My own contribution to environmental biology was both callow and obstreperous, nurtured by exciting primary school trips to the Kruger National Park (I do hope school children today get the chance to enjoy them; they were priceless). The time of which I write was long ago, and so the only game in town was "guess the animal". By Standard Five we knew most of them, although no one back then paid much attention to the birds (excepting perhaps for Robin, who went on to become one of the country's leading ornithologists; from small eggs and all that).

We were each required to buy a Kruger Park guidebook which, back then, cost about a rand. A surprising number of kids invested the money in provisions instead. For that amount you could buy a bagful of goodies: cooldrink – 10 cents (deposit 2 1/2 cents), packet chips – 5 cents, Creamy Toffee – 5 cents, small chocolate bar – 5 cents, fruit gums – 5 cents, fruit drops – 2 1/2 cents, Wicks bubblegum – 1 cent, Chappies bubblegum – ½ cent. Times were sweet.

The guidebooks then were pretty simple compared with the virtual libraries and apps available today. Back then each animal got a page, including a wash-style illustration and information about general appearance, size, if they occurred singly or in groups, a few words on food, voice or call: things like behaviour, habitat and status were concepts of a time yet to come. And gestation period. They all included gestation period: we had to look it up and there wasn't even Google back then. You had to go to an actual library.

The teacher would commend you for each fact you could trot out. Being one of the obtuse kids, I took it upon myself to memorise the gestation periods of all the animals. The task was greatly simplified once I worked out there was a correlation between size and term of pregnancy – elephant (645 days), impala (200 days), gerbil (24 days). Also, between them and the size of their poop.

Each time the teacher pointed to an animal, up would shoot my hand.

"Yeees, David?"

"Giraffe, gestation period 15 months."

I could be really exasperating; it's a wonder I reached maturity.

Obviously guidebook information back then was gleaned from what scant animal research there was available at the time, meshed in with old hunting lore. And you know what tall tales a hunter will recount around the glowing embers once mugs have been refilled.

Turns out many hunters didn't really know that much about nature in general, so focused were they on shooting the Big Five, breeding tracking dogs and making biltong. For example, I remember my guidebook said giraffes did not live in herds (or they were loose and fluctuating ones) and did not vocalise: both of which turned out to be wrong (although, to be fair, it was never obvious and took a new generation of animal behaviouralists to discover).

So what do we know about them now? Turns out still not very much at all. We do know they are tall, they are stately, and mostly still and generally so tranquil they are often overlooked on the expansive African landscape. They seem not to jostle, to bicker or to fuss. And yet in many ways they are the most unexpected and beautiful of all wild creatures.

Sometimes it takes time and the accumulated knowledge across many fields of inquiry to find out what really makes a thing tick, or tock. For example, modern animal behavioural studies have revealed that giraffes have matriachal herds, much like elephants, but do not stick as tightly together. The voice is another story: it's a long one, about twice the length of a giraffe's neck, so get comfortable...

INVARIABLY SCHOOLYARDS THE WORLD OVER are beset by fatuous arguments: Flake or Tex bar, marbles or hopscotch, hip-hop or R&B, Pink Floyd or Radiohead, Beyoncé or Swift, Hendrix or ... (in the case of James Marshall Hendrix there is no "or".) We grow up and realise these are all inconclusive debates which, unfortunately, sometimes escape the playground and make for irksome dinner-table conversations (Beatles or Stones, Chenin or Chardonnay).

Some more cerebral debates over the years have included the likes of Galileo Galilei versus the Roman Catholic Church (Sun goes round

Earth, Earth around Sun), Fred Hoyle and Albert Einstein (steady state universe, or an expanding "big bang" one), Charles Darwin and God (evolution or creation).

One that particularly interests me is the ongoing palaver generated by the works of Richard Dawkins (Oxford professor of evolutionary biology) and Stephen Jay Gould (Harvard professor of palaeontology, obit 2002). I suspect there will be no winner in this one, since they seem to be arguing the same thing looking in opposite directions. Kind of like trying to discern the nature of things when one person is looking through a telescope and the other through a microscope.

The Dawkins-Gould debate[13] centres on the question: what is the essential driver of evolution? Dawkins comes at the debate from his expertise in conventional Darwinian evolutionary biology, which is a – relatively – short-term viewpoint (microscope). Gould is, or was, a geologist and palaeontologist, which offers the very long-term view of things (telescope).

Dawkins holds that evolution advances in short fits and long starts (punctuated equilibrium), which helps to explain events like past mass extinctions, as well as biological mushrooming, the most notable of which is (or was) the Cambrian Explosion around 500 mya. At the laboratories analysing the Burgess Shales from Banff in Canada, in which the Cambrian period fossils were first found, there was an in-joke. Each time a new slab of shale was prised apart someone would groan: "Oh no, not another @#$% phylum!"[14]

The Gould model of all things proposes that there is an overall steady rate of continual change to DNA structures among all living organisms. It protests that Dawkins's "short fits and long starts" view is too limited and does not average out the observed (palaeontological) reality that life has developed slowly and ceaselessly from "lower" bacterial life forms through increasingly "higher" ones: bacteria > fungi > plants > invertebrates (jellyfish)

---

[13] The full story can be found in *Survival of the Fittest* by Kim Sterelny, Icon Books, Cambridge UK, 2001/2007

[14] A phylum is a fairly high level in the classification of life, lying between order and kingdom. There are just six phyla: animal, plant, fungi (mushrooms and the like), protista (amoeba), bacteria and archaea (single-celled things that lack nuclei, also prokaryotes).

> vertebrates (fish, insects) > amphibians > reptiles > birds > mammals > us. Just look at the fossil record in the rocks, it's been written there over the past 3.2 billion years.

Insiders refer to the two models as "evolution by jerks" and "evolution by creeps" and it really is a Beatles-Stones debate, since each viewpoint illustrates different aspects of evolution. Leaning over towards the geo camp, I tend to hang with Gould and the "creeps" hypothesis, but with some wiggle room for things like the Cambrian Explosion. Not least because he was arguably the most erudite and entertaining writer of popular earth sciences the world has known.

But I have to acknowledge a grudging admiration for Dawkins. His books such as *The Selfish Gene* and *The Blind Watchmaker* (among some 30 titles) helped to spell out and popularise the great evolutionary debate – and raise huge controversy along the way in both scientific and lay circles. Like, if God had submitted his design for the human eye as a first-year bioengineering project, he would have failed miserably.

I particularly like Dawkins for the TV series "Inside Nature's Giants" in which he, along with a panel of experts, conducts post-mortem dissections on a variety of very large animals. The finback whale, second in size to the blue, that washed up on a beach of County Cork, Ireland, yielded a heart the size of a small motorcar. The deceased zoo lion revealed the most amazing larynx of any animal, able to retract deep into its chest, which accounts for that decibel-topping roar.

It was hard to choose a favourite animal necropsy between the likes of Nile crocodile, great white shark, elephant, hippo, camel, leatherback turtle, thoroughbred racehorse (Flake, Tex, Bar One, Toff-o-Lux, Kit-Kat …). For me it was the giraffe (and Tex), for what it revealed about evolution over time, and what the long neck has meant in terms of behaviour.

First was that it had a huge heart, more than 10 kilograms in weight (compared with ours at between 0.2 to 0.3 kilograms), in order to pump some 60 litres of blood (we have just 10 or 11) through those long legs, up its long neck and to the brain. Its blood pressure is the highest of any animal (twice ours). To protect its brain from sudden changes in blood pressure when bending to drink and then lifting itself upright – often with a sudden flick of the neck – it has special valves inside extra-elasticised blood vessels.

All of which is super interesting, but not the most interesting yet. Most fascinating (for me at least) is what that long neck has done for its speech, or lack thereof. To gain the full picture we have to go far back in time, to when fish ruled and there were no land animals anywhere (around 300 mya or so). To start with, fish had no external ears, and still don't.

How hearing works for them is that their bodies are about the same density as the water in which they swim. Inside, behind their gills, is a bone called an otolith that is denser than both fish and water. The otolith is surrounded by little hairs, called cilia. As the fish moves, the difference in density between the rest of its body and the otolith sets up a wave, which vibrates the cilia, joined to the brain by a nerve, which the brain detects as "sound".

As fish begat amphibians and amphibians begat reptiles then mammal-like reptiles, one of the changes that occurred was that gills became ears. All this time, while land animals developed necks, the nerve that originally connected a fish's gills to its brain lengthened, evolved into its vocal cord nerve which, during the process, got "trapped" under the aortic arch in the chest. Notch it up as another of the Creator's less successful designs.

The recurrent laryngeal (voice) nerve of a giraffe must run from its larynx (voice box), all the way down into its chest, loop under its heart, then return back up the neck to its cerebellum. That nerve is about as thick as your thumb and feels like marrow jelly. In a typical adult giraffe that's a journey of around five metres.

For us this laryngeal nerve thing is not such a big deal, since our hearts are located only about 40 centimetres from our brains, yakety yakety yak. It turns out that giraffes are mostly silent because it's just so hard for them to vibrate their vocal cords, what with a 2.3-metre-long trachea linked to that unnervingly long laryngeal nerve.

But that does not mean they do not vocalise at all. They have been recorded grunting and snorting when alarmed, bleating when in distress, bellowing when hungry, mooing when lonely and whistling to attract their young. But what they do mostly, researchers have found, is hum. We can't hear it because it's subsonic to humans, and they do it mostly at night. I like to think they are communicating with giraffe music.

Right now there is no agreement as to how many species of giraffe there are. Even over the past few decades it's gone from several to one, to three, four and even eight. Seven or eight seems to be the current thinking. For interest's sake they are, or might be: Kordofan from Central-West Africa; Nubian, Rothchild's and Masai from East Africa; West African or Nigerian; Reticulated or Somalian; Thornicroft's from Zambia's Luangwa Valley; South or Southern African; and Angolan.

PROBABLY THE MOST FAMOUS OF its kind was a "tall horse" named Zarafa, a female Nubian giraffe sent as a gift from Sultan Mohammed Ali of Egypt to King Charles of France, at what turned out to be a most inexpedient time.[15] It arrived at Marseilles in 1825, a time when post-revolutionary feelings were running at fever pitch.

The unfortunate animal was marched to Paris as a kind of royal curiosity (just think of those Parisian winters, after Sudan!). All along the route the approaching cavalcade caused great emotions and drew large crowds in holiday spirits. There were also tense philosophical debates about whether this fantastical creature was a revolutionary or a reactionary one. Should it be fêted or flambéed? The French are like that. It lived to 1845 and some say it was the inspiration for the Eiffel Tower.

Although giraffes are mostly serene and reticent, that is not always the case. Males of the species are like most males out there in the jungle: defending territories and sparring for mating rights. If you've seen two males having a go at one another it appears to be happening in slow motion so you might assume not much damage could be done.

---

[15] The tale of "Tall Horse" was told on stage with a life-size giraffe marionette made by the Handspring Puppet Company of Cape Town, which also made the horses for "War Horse". Seeing three people working the giraffe from the inside remains one of the most mesmerising dramatisations I have ever witnessed. The inspired script was written by Afro-American writer Khefra Burns.

However, if you know something about physics, you can only imagine what kind of force can be generated through the big bony head at the end of its slingshot neck. When hammered against the chest or leg of the opponent, the horny protrusions – called ossicones – can generate rib-cracking or even heart-stopping blows.

Also, in places such as the South African Lowveld where they are among the favoured prey of lions, their soup-plate feet can deliver a fatal blow to an incautious predator. If ever you've seen a lion or lioness with its jaw all askance, the most likely cause was a blow from a giraffe's hoof.

Their tongues are also very long, 45 centimetres or more, and they are dark purple, which you would know if you'd ever watched one feeding, delicately stripping fine, compound branchlets. It's thought the deep colouration is some kind of shield against sunburn, given that their tongues are hung out there, on the top of the tree canopy, through the heat of the day.

Together with the extraordinary tongue and tough, prehensile lips, a giraffe's mouth works like a very tough human hand. It is absorbing watching one feeding as it picks the feathery leaves of their favoured acacia plants from between needle- or razor-sharp thorns, with surprisingly dexterity.

These slow-walking ruminants feed for up to 18 hours a day, consuming up to 30 kilograms of leaves, fresh shoots, sometimes along with the vines that climb around the canopies, even occasionally chewing bones for a calcium supplement. They have, like us, a full complement of 32 teeth, excepting in place of the front ones on top they form a hard plate against which leaves can be stripped.

A giraffe walks into a café. It orders a coffee and a sandwich, eats it, then draws a pistol and shoots the waiter when she presents the bill.

"But why?" pleads the bleeding server, as the animal makes for the exit.

"I'm a giraffe," it turns and says (stooping), "Google it."

In a last, dying action the waiter takes out her mobile, enters "giraffe" and reads:

Giraffe, mammal, native to Africa. Eats, shoots & leaves.

A Most Propitious Paddle: The Saga of a Hippo, a Crocodile, a Buffalo and Some Very Fortunate Humans

A PHOTOJOURNALIST COLLEAGUE OF MINE, also named David, was sitting round the campfire at Tena Tena tented safari camp in Zambia's South Luangwa National Park, telling the gathered guests about his colleague's (my) recent escape from the jaws of a hippo on the upper Zambezi River. They all *oohed* and *aahed* at the appropriate moments, including a man who sported impressive scars that looked like he'd recently done battle with a dragon.

Another of the guests, Alex, turned to this middle-aged fellow, a Zambezi River safari operator, and said: "Why don't you tell them about your recent encounter, Alistair?" And so began the tale of what must surely be one of the most incredible incidents of attack and survival that has ever been shared around an African fire.

Alistair Gellatly was an avid fisher and one fine day in 1994 found him taking two of his friends, a married couple, as well as the wife's parents, out from England, on a grand adventure to share with them a slice of his life in the bush. Fishing lines were out and given that the sun was creeping upwards towards the yardarm (which, as you'll know, on a motorboat is famously low) the picnic basket had been opened and chilled Zambezis, the preferred local brew, passed around.

The host was nonchalant about the worrying number of large crocodiles sunning on sandbanks, the hippos that snorted as the boat drifted past, and the elephants that waded into the shallows to drink, feast on soft water plants and generally cool down. He'd been a safari guide most of his adult life and this was just another day on the river.

No sooner had one of the party yelled that they had the first bite of a tigerfish on their line than the sound of a thunderous hammer blow hit the aluminium hull and shook it vigorously. Two of the party fell overboard, while on the opposite side of the boat the ivory yellow tusks of a massive bull hippo raked the length of the boat.

Those still aboard held on for their all, but to no avail. The next moment the beast upended the boat completely, leaving the entire party thrashing for their lives in the mighty Zambezi River. Extremely lucky for them the old bull, having asserted its dominion over its section of the river, moved away.

Others in similar situations on the river have not been so lucky in the event of a hippo lunge, the animal known to have killed many people, including safari guides or their guests, on this well-paddled waterway. We'll hear about one of the luckier ones in good time.

The group linked arms as they were carried about 60 metres downstream by the powerful current, delivering them onto a submerged sandbar where they could stand, about knee-deep in the swirling water. The rest of the party looked to Alistair, as if to say: "So, what's the plan, bush master?"

The old safari hand knew he'd find both fishing and canoeing camps on the Zimbabwean side of the river, but that would entail a swim of about a kilometre. Much closer was the Zambian bank, about 100 metres away. On that side he would find only indigenous villages, but with luck he would be able to shout or otherwise signal across the river for assistance.

Given that the crocodiles (otherwise known as flat dogs in that part of the world) were mostly dozing in the heat of the day, he reckoned that would be their best chance. Once the sun began its descent the giant reptiles would start to get active and return to the river, so the sooner he set off the better. He swam for the Zambian shore while the current continued to pull him downstream. You can almost imagine the scene, like a latter-day Captain Oates setting out into the unknown: "Excuse me gentlemen, ladies, I may be some time…"

Alistair made for a narrow inlet, since the bank along there was otherwise vertical and was some metres high. Just as the reluctant triathlete (drinkin' and fishin' and swimmin') was approaching the riverbank he noticed the prehistoric form of a large crocodile slip off the bank and slide underwater – not a huge one, but big enough to indicate that if it came to it, he'd nonetheless be in for the fight of his life.

The man paddled himself backwards into clearer water, slapping the surface to try to dissuade an attack, then ducked under, the better to prepare himself for the reptile's inevitable approach. He saw it coming for him like a scaly torpedo. Alistair lifted his legs and the attacker brushed the undersides of his feet as it swept past. But it turned immediately and came again, smacking the man in his back with its powerful tail and winding him.

He sucked air into his lungs and submerged again, in anticipation of the next attack. Within moments the crocodile's cast-iron jaws clamped around his upper body and began to drag him into deeper water. Alistair managed to free one arm, which prompted to crocodile to tear at his right arm and torso, and spin him at the same time.

The six-foot, 100-kilogram prey felt bones in his right arm snap and tendons tear, elbow and shoulder dislocated. The croc released its grip in order to get a firmer hold, so as to spin and rip its prey apart (for the same anatomical reasons they cannot chew but rip off and swallow chunks while holding their breaths). This gave Alistair a very brief window to retaliate. He locked his legs around the reptile's body and, remembering conversations about how to fight a crocodile, punched its snout – managing only to damage his hand.

So he jabbed fingers into its eyes (another bit of bush folklore), but that seemed to have no better effect. All the time the two were locked in mortal combat and heading into deeper water. Using all his strength he tried to bend one of the croc's supposedly weak front claws, only to find that "weak" in a mature crocodile is a relative thing. Clearly all those buggers around all those fires over the years who'd spoken with such authority about how to fight a flat dog had never actually tried. Meanwhile, the monster kept on shaking the man as if he were a rag doll, and blood was staining the water around them.

By now the victim was running out of air and had just seconds in which to deliver some incredible life-saving blow, or die. Think of James Bond strapped, legs apart, to a sliding bench and inching towards a band saw… But Alistair did in fact have one more secret-agent move. Crocodiles do not have the hard palate mammals do, so when tearing into prey, they rely on a flap of flesh at the back of their throat to keep water from entering their lungs.

Alistair rammed his good arm down its throat and felt for that flap. He touched a rubbery appendage (the palatal valve), all the while feeling brutal teeth shredding his flesh. But he got a hold of it and pulled and twisted like his life depended on it. Which of course it did.

This caused the crocodile to take water into its lungs. Its jaws opened as it spluttered, releasing its prey. Using the bits that still worked, Alistair splashed his way to the shore, dragged himself onto dry land and lay there gasping and heaving, alive but shattered and bleeding. He managed to concoct a tourniquet and sling using his shirt and a stick, and then continued on his mission to rescue his stricken fishing mates.

As he recalled years later, he did manage to shout to them that he'd been attacked by a croc, but that he would press on to try to find help. He made it barely to the high-water mark before blacking out. Meanwhile, the party in the river realised the cavalry would not be coming any time soon.

Next thing he remembers was that it was getting dark and creatures of the night had begun to stir. Working as best he could, he piled stones around his feet. First he heard lions calling, then later, and even closer, hyenas. Not only had he left a blood trail, but also this would be the first night he'd have to endure in the bush without a firearm, alone.

While drifting in and out of sleep, or consciousness, he noted everything had gone silent, then next moment there was a loud snort close by. That was followed by heavy breathing and equally heavy footsteps – and then the massive span of curved horns and hefty boss of a big old buffalo bull appeared out of the gloom.

Knowing well the fearsome reputation of belligerent old loner "dagha boys", Alistair threw sticks and stones in the hope of chasing it away. Undaunted it advanced slowly, stopped about 10 metres away, crossed its front legs, grunted and lay down. The man, and indeed everyone who has ever heard his story, cannot figure out why, but that old bull stayed sentinel all night and watched over the stricken man, very possibly saving his life.

When he awoke at dawn Alistair found he was alone, alive, but in poor shape. In the distance, silhouetted against the mirror-shine of the low sunlight on the river, he counted four figures: his people had survived their own night of terror. There was no time to waste, so he set off following the riverbank, but with no certainty in what direction.

Lucky for him, sometime later he saw fishers in a boat on the river and within a short time his stranded party was scooped up by a motorboat and taken safely, both stirred and shaken, to shore. But that's only his side of the story; the other is about what happened to the good folk left literally knee-deep in the river.

As the sun lowered itself onto the Zambian escarpment the party of four realised, or at least one of them did – Arthur, an experienced hunter – that without any means of defence they would become easy prey for the multitude of crocodiles around them. And that was when he spied a blue and silver paddle floating towards them. Throwing caution overboard he waded into deeper water to retrieve the god-sent weapon.

And true to type, as darkness descended so too did the crocodiles. It must have been the longest night of any of their souls, spent in its entirety fending off lunging beasts. Some of the more emboldened ones had to be beaten repeatedly about their heads to keep them at bay. All night they could see the moonlight reflect the deep red dots of reptilian eyes encircling them, waiting, as crocodiles are so adept at doing.

At the same time that the Gellatly party set off on their fishing caper (it was an Easter long weekend), river guide Phil Longden was leading a group of German tourists on a canoe trip down the lower Zambezi. They were on a lazy section of the river when Longden suggested they do a "leg over" and float with the current past an island where antelope and buffaloes were grazing, with linen white egrets darting between their legs to snap up insects as they were flushed by the herbivores' feet.

As they were floating in tropical stupor, a hippo burst out of a nearby reed bed and charged the peaceful flotilla. Phil knew they were in mortal danger and he shouted to his group to disentangle their legs and push their canoes apart ASA bloody well P. As the guide was kicking off from the canoe alongside, the hippo clamped its ferocious jaws on his leg.

Phil did his best to beat the enraged animal with his paddle in an attempt to escape, but it pulled him clear of the canoe and dragged him underwater. In the ensuing struggle the guide lost his paddle. The terrified German tourists instinctively beat the water with their own paddles.

It worked and the hippopotamus let go of the river guide and retreated back to its lair in the reeds. Phil surfaced and was pulled aboard one of the canoes, then rowed to shore where medical assistance was sought. They set off first for the Zimbabwean side of the river but, failing to locate anything resembling civilisation, headed over to the Zambian side. It took from late morning till after dark to locate a safari camp capable of arranging for Phil's evacuation.

His leg was a mess, completely mangled and with the bits above and below the knee being held together by threads of body tissue. Due to the delay in receiving prompt expert medical treatment, it was found later that gangrene had set in and the leg below the knee had to be amputated. It was some two days after the attack on Longden's group that his double-bladed paddle floated close to another beleaguered group on – or really in – the river.

Meanwhile, back on the riverbank a critically injured Alistair Gellatly had been stumbling along the riverbank for several hours. A reconstruction of events suggests he managed to make no more than a few hundred metres' headway before coming alongside a boat of Zimbabwean fishers drifting along without a care. Unable to shout, he waved at them. They waved back.

Then, realising that a white man alone on the wild riverbank where no white man ought to be was something to be investigated, they did. Within no time they'd taken him to their tent camp, tended his wounds as best they could, then set out in their boat to collect his exhausted companions still stranded in the middle of the river.

But still that was not quite the end of the ordeal. The first plane dispatched to collect Gellatly landed well enough on a nearby bush strip but (for reasons never specified) was thereafter unable to execute a take-off. Eventually a second aeroplane was enlisted and it did manage a proficient landing followed by a successful take-off, destination: hospital in Harare.

A year later, scars and skin grafts healing well enough, he thought to visit his mates, the Shentons, who ran Tena Tena in the South Luangwa valley (the Luangwa River is the major tributary of the lower Zambezi and has, it is rumoured, the highest density of hippos and crocodiles in Southern Africa). I wonder how many times, around how many fires, this story has been told, and how many times those who've heard it have done the same. So, given the multiplying effect, it's surprising you had not heard it before.

Women in the Wilderness: Sisters are Doing It for Themselves

WHERE TO BEGIN THIS STORY of women who have dedicated their working lives to nature? There are sure to be others of whom we know less, but among the pioneers were Americans such as Hallie Daggett. As a youngster at the turn of the 19th century, she learned all the skills of what is still referred to as backwoodsman stuff like tracking, trapping, hunting, fishing and building log cabins. This skillset led to her being drafted as the first female employee of the US Forest Service.

Around the same time Herma Baggley became the first woman assigned a field job in the US National Park Service, where she was a pioneer in botany and nature education in Yellowstone. Like Daggett, she helped pave the way for later appointments of women to top posts in both organisations – although some decades later.

Then there is Rachel Carson, born in 1907, who died in 1964. She worked for the US Fish and Wildlife Service back when most of us were either still stardust or learning cursive writing. She resigned to write full time, turning her work into the game-changing book *Silent Spring*. It opened the world's eyes to wide-scale agricultural poisoning, ensuring she is remembered as the "mother of the environmental movement" worldwide.

The serious conversation about women working with African wildlife begins in Hampstead, London, when Mr and Mrs Morris-Goodall gave their daughter Jane a stuffed toy chimpanzee, which she named Jubilee. The relatives were concerned the "creature" would frighten the slight young lass, but instead it engendered in her a lifelong fondness for wild animals.

That fondness led her to a friend's farm in Africa when she was in her early twenties. There, a chance meeting with the world's leading paleoanthropologist of the time, Louis Leakey, secured her a job as his secretary (actually the friend had engineered the whole thing). By degrees Leakey steered the young wannabe primate researcher to Gombe Stream National Park. The warden insisted an older person accompany her, so her mother joined young Jane. I've been to Gombe and concur it's a really remote and wild place, on the shore of Lake Tanganyika; the kind of place you would be happy to have a reliable companion.

Five years later Goodall earned a PhD from Cambridge University – one of only nine people to be awarded a doctorate without first having completed an undergraduate degree there. Her thesis was entitled "Behaviour of Free-Living Chimpanzees", the first of its kind in English. To keep things honest, a team of Japanese primatologists had got there before her and the University of Kyoto maintains a team of primatologists at Gombe.

Goodall's work dovetailed very well with Leakey's, who was looking at the evolution of hominins in East Africa and wanted to know more about the great apes. Today, Goodall is considered the world's foremost authority on chimpanzees; she is an international conservation champion, and carries the title Dame (and was also formerly a baroness by virtue of her marriage to Dutch wildlife filmmaker Baron Hugo von Lawick). Jubilee still lives with her.

Next on the scene, also at Leakey's behest, was a prickly American woman named Dian Fossey. In 1966 she set up camp at Karisoke in Rwanda's Volcanoes National Park, to study mountain gorillas. Her work was hugely successful, but the area was in the grip of civil strife that would dog her research and her personal life till the end.

The gorillas became, effectively, family to her and when poachers moved in and started killing them for bush meat and trophies (apparently gorilla heads and hands made excellent curios for foreign visitors), Fossey began her own guerrilla war against them. After 20 years of ground-breaking work, Fossey was found murdered in her cabin. Although an American research assistant was convicted of the crime in absentia, many people believe her death was at the hands of local poachers.

Fossey's life in Africa began after she had cashed in her life savings to go on safari in East Africa. While visiting the Leakey family's archaeological dig site at Olduvai Gorge in the Serengeti ecosystem, she met patriarch Louis. He needed more work to be done on the great apes and so Fossey became the second of what came to be known as the "trimates": three women who studied the great apes and each became a world authority in their own rights. The other being Biruté Galdikas who has become known as the world champion of orangutans, working with them in Borneo and Malaysia.

ANOTHER NAME THAT WILL BE familiar to many is Joy Adamson. Some time ago I had the chance to spend a few days at Elsa's Kopje safari lodge in Kenya's Meru National Park, where her ashes were scattered. The lodge has the complete collection of both Joy and George Adamson's books (about a dozen in all), and I spent a day there speed-reading them. Such remarkable people and what stories!

Joy was born in what was then the Austro-Hungarian Empire, in a region we now call the Czech Republic, on a hunting estate. She earned a music degree at Vienna and soon after married the first of three husbands, Victor von Klarwill. Being Jewish, and it being the mid-1930s, he wisely decided they should relocate to British East Africa, sending his new wife ahead. Not so wisely for him though, because on the ship she had an affair with English botanist and artist Peter Bally, whom she married sometime later. But the marriage did not endure and she embarked on a number of affairs, specifically with rugged game ranger-hunter types.

At a New Year's Eve party in Nairobi in 1943 she met the hirsute, sun-weathered game warden George Adamson. His job at the time was to patrol and protect the extremely remote and rugged Northern Range territory; he must have scrubbed up really well for the party because otherwise he seldom wore much other than shorts and veldskoens. Joy followed him there, and was more than happy living under canvas with George and his askaris.

One fateful day in 1956, while George was out on patrol, a lioness rushed at him from a crevice in a koppie and the warden was forced to shoot it at close range. He discovered she had been protecting three cubs, which he took back to camp. Three was more than they could manage, so two were sent to the Rotterdam Zoo. The third, a female they named Elsa, became the famous protagonist of their lives for several years and later the book, movie and hit song *Born Free*.

Once Joy achieved fame as both a writer and artist of great merit (she was commissioned by the Kenyan government to paint all the ethnic groups of the country and also amassed a considerable collection of botanical illustrations) the couple drifted apart but never divorced. Joy had a string of younger lovers and worked with leopards and cheetahs, while George continued to live among the lions at Meru.

They did, however, spend each Christmas together for the rest of their lives. Joy Adamson was murdered in 1980 in Shaba National Reserve by a young employee. Not long after George was machine-gunned by Somali shiftas (cattle rustlers and poachers) nine years later while saving the life of a tourist near his camp at Kora, not far from Meru (cue *Born Free* theme song).

In Southern Africa the change from white men's only club in the wildlife and tourism business became noticeable in the 1990s, largely as a result of various nature conservation and game ranger courses being offered school leavers. Most women graduating from these courses tended to find employment in the various provincial nature conservation departments in South Africa, but then increasingly at private game reserves and lodges across the region.

Only recently the Kruger National Park appointed its first woman head ranger, Cathy Dreyer: notable not only as the first woman, but also the first one of colour. In times not so long past, even with her exceptional credentials in spearheading black rhino conservation in both the Kruger and Addo Elephant national parks, as well as in the Great Fish Nature Reserve in the Eastern Cape, Dreyer almost certainly would have hit a low-thatch career ceiling.

It is foolish to hold that anyone was the first to do pretty much anything: like, who was the first person to make a fire, or who was

Women in the Wilderness: Sisters are Doing It for Themselves

the first woman game guide in Africa? We'll never know for sure, but Wilderness Safaris – started by two bushy-tailed lads with an old Land Rover back in 1983 and now Africa's largest safari operator – was among the first to negotiate proper land leases with indigenous people for their safari camps, persistently employ local people and, wherever possible, upskill them and promote them up the ranks.

Around 20 years ago there was hardly a handful of women game guides and rangers across Africa, but today you would not be aware there had ever been discrimination in the ranks. In fact, if you booked at Chobe Game Lodge you might wonder where all the rugged great white hunters of old had gone: the place employs only female guides who call themselves the Chobe Angels. Asilia Africa's Dunia safari camp in Tanzania's Serengeti National Park has gone one step further: the entire staff, cleaners, guides and managers are women.

Bear in mind these camps are for the most part found in areas of Africa where male chauvinism is deeply entrenched. And yet, whether it's Botswana, Namibia, South Africa, Tanzania or Rwanda, the sight of highly qualified women game guides, wildlife researchers or game rangers hefting assault rifles hardly warrants a comment.

IF YOU SHOULD FIND YOURSELF slipping and sliding on the steep, densely forested slopes of a volcano in Rwanda on your way to find gorillas, you might have chanced upon Aline Umutoni at the head of a crocodile of young people, out for a nature ramble around the lower reaches. She heads the country's Children in the Wilderness programme, an initiative of Wilderness Safaris in areas where it has a presence. During the year the safari company raises funds for the programme, then closes select camps to paying guests for a period each year, hosting children from local communities on wildlife, environmental and life-skills camps.

That you might meet Aline there at all is something of a wonder. She was a child when civil war ravaged her country, ending in a bloody holocaust that left a trail of blood and death, brutalising and displacing countless millions – of which she was one. When she returned to her native land it was with a degree in forestry and nature conservation, bolstered by a diploma in wildlife management.

That landed her a job at Volcanoes National Park guiding visitors on nature walks, what the safari world calls gorilla trekking.

However, all things there were not going well. The place had been used as a military hideout during the war, following which impoverished local people began stripping the forests back to make fields, while poachers were hard at work in what remained. The volcanoes area straddles the borders of Rwanda, Democratic of Congo and Uganda and is the last refuge of mountain gorillas. Around two decades ago there was an estimated 700 to 800 of them surviving in their beleaguered habitat (where Dian Fossey had begun her work, researching and conserving the bulky great apes).

Into this scenario parachuted the safari company, buying farmland on the lower slopes, employing and reskilling the local people, replanting forest and starting a tourism hub that would, in time, they hoped, help to extend the national park and also develop the region economically and socially.

To date more than 50 000 trees have been planted and wildlife is beginning to follow the down-slope expansion. At the time of writing the wild population of gorillas was estimated to be around 1 060, and for the first time in decades gorillas were seen (on camera trap), walking around the expanded forest area around Bisate.

When the company opened its Bisate Lodge, now among the most desirable safari destinations in Africa, the national parks trail guide was an obvious asset for them to head hunt. In 2017, when the lodge opened, Aline was both its activities coordinator and senior guide. With that job came the opportunity to visit safari lodges in other countries in order to further her know-how.

Two years later found her as the face of Children in the Wilderness at Bisate, responsible for raising funds, liaising with around 1 000 families that live around the lodge and park, implementing community projects such as solar light installations, blanket distribution, providing hardware and internet access at Bisate Primary School, mentoring eco-clubs in tree-planting, and of course leading the local youth into the forest to see what lives up there.

In 2021, Aline Umutoni was recognised by the World Wide Fund for Nature (WWF) as one of Africa's top 100 young conservationists.

Doing what she does, where she does it, determines that what she does goes far beyond the conventional understanding of a job. That has included organising and distributing food parcels to help the local people through the Covid tourism drought. Hers has become a life and a calling, shining a light up the cloud-swathed mountains and giving thousands of young people sight of a bright future.

On receiving her award, she said: "I am so proud to work for a company that keeps supporting the people most in need. Since I started working there in 2017, I have witnessed first-hand how lives are changed and how we make a difference."

It's amazing who you might meet in a pub, and where a chance meeting might lead you. In the case of Theresa Dunn (Diane Keaton) in the movie *Looking for Mister Goodbar* it did not end well at all. However, in the case of Emsie Verwey it led her down a twisting desert trail in a place where the horizon is an ever-moving mirage. I did not ask her what pub it was, but I'd bet it was Kücki's in Swakopmund which, along with the Duck Inn in Maun, is your typical tavern at the edge of the known universe.

On leaving school she first worked at a photographic laboratory in Swakopmund, where she grew up. She says every day the world beyond came to her in the images she developed, and along with them the bush characters who brought "dust, wood smoke and sweat". The lure of the wilds became increasingly enticing to her, living in a small town enclosed by harsh desert.

As it happened, the bloke she met turned out to be one of Southern Africa's legendary guides, a veritable local Crocodile Dundee. From her hometown, sandwiched between desert and ocean, she followed said fellow to a safari camp deep in the Namib Desert where he worked at the time. She's never left, although said bushman moved on. At age 24 she found herself in charge of a luxe bush lodge sans telephones, wi-fi, mobile phone connection or internet. Entertainment was listening in on the bush radio to the local news and gossip.

"Very quickly I had to learn a *lot* about running a camp," she tells me, "from housekeeping and plumbing to managing stock, menus, maintenance and mechanics, but also working as a liaison officer with the surrounding communities whose land we basically leased." Also on occasion having to clear snakes out of guest rooms. "Although some of it was very routine, most of the time you never knew what the day would bring.

"I met a lot of people and attended a lot of meetings under camelthorn trees in the vast northwest of Namibia," she recalls. It was there she was exposed to research and conservation for the first time: "People with great vision, a history with the land and the people. It was very stimulating and a privilege to be a part of that."

She recollected how she assisted with the relocation of black rhinos, as well as lion relocation operations. "It made a big impact on this small-town girl. I could not believe my luck sometimes: seeing a rhino suspended upside down from a helicopter flying over the mountains of the Kaokoveld is a sight I will never forget."

It was while working with the Desert Lion Conservation Trust that her life took its next turn. She recounts how she knew "something" about brown hyenas, but they had always been out of sight and out of mind. This is the animal known in those parts as the strandjutwolf, an animal that local lore associates with secrecy and death.

The first one she ever saw appeared like a spectre out of the mist in the bed of the Khumib River: "I was terrified." Later two staff members told her they'd seen "two small brown things" running around outside a hole on a nearby mountain. Lured by what they might be, she set up a camera trap outside the hole.

The camera trap took stills as well as some video clips and the "two brown things" turned out to be brown hyena cubs and now she is the region's foremost researcher of brown hyenas. "To this day, I still remember the first time I saw the female come to the den, call the cubs and then suckle them. I started going to the den in the mornings and watched the cubs grow up."

A not so small hurdle was that very little information was available at the time about brown hyenas in general, and even more so those of the Skeleton Coast. However, by continual monitoring of the camera traps she started learning how to recognise individuals, what food was brought back to the den … but then the camp at which she was working was closed and so a curtain came down on her work.

Luckily it was re-opened a few years later, and when Emsie returned to the den she found not only was it still active but it was still being used by the same females she'd first seen there. "This really cemented my passion and slight brown hyena obsession," she jokes. That's also when, with encouragement from lion researcher Dr Philip (Flip) Stander, she started collecting her own data on the brown hyenas of the Skeleton Coast.

The new dispensation allowed her to monitor three clans in the Hoanib valley, as well as locating others in the Swakopmund, Ugab, Huab and Khoigab valleys, along with one at Terrace Bay and another at a place called Toscanini (I have no idea, maybe an Italian opera singer whose body washed up on the Skeleton Coast).

She says she hopes, and expects, to be there for the next 10 to 15 years as the "small baseline study" grows into the most sustained study of these endangered animals. They are listed as "near threatened" on the IUCN Red Data List, with only an estimated 7 000 living across Mozambique, South Africa, Zimbabwe, Botswana and Namibia.

A large part of her work is educating people about the elusive and harmless animals, which are nevertheless persecuted by humans in rural areas, fearing them as creatures of the darkness. Emsie calls them her "wolfies", pronounced the Afrikaans way (volfies). Her new title at Hoanib is no longer camp gofer but Field Based Research Coordinator for Hoanib Skeleton Coast Camp. Cheers to that.

THE GRASS CEILING FOR MOST women in Africa is perilously close to rock bottom. Many of those I encountered while researching this chapter had similar sagas to tell: hard labour, often child labour, not much if any education, forced marriages, rape, you name it. There are few rights in their world, only responsibilities. It's therefore humbling to meet someone who has clawed her way out of a seemingly hopeless hole to the top of the world, or close to.

Following a lead from Tanzanian "super guide" Pietro Luraschi, I tracked down Glory Salema in Arusha, the jump-off town for trekking on Kilimanjaro. The story she told me was so moving, possibly because I have met her, or one of her mountain sisters, up on those frigid slopes.

She was born in 1988 on a small holding at the foot of Mount Kilimanjaro, she writes to me in reply to my request for her story. Her parents were farmers – but since the plot they farmed was about 10 kilometres from their home, each day's toil included a long walk. When she was still young she and her younger siblings would be left with her grandparents who lived nearby.

"When I was nine I began to follow my parents to the farm, but since we did not have transport I had to walk the long distance, through the bush and often in the dark all by myself. Sometimes she would hear hyenas calling. One time her father had a close encounter with a leopard (miso).

"My childhood was not easy," she says matter-of-factly. "I can still remember people called me a boy because I played soccer and could climb trees. I can ride a bicycle, and when a girl rides a bike here, they say she can lose her virginity. Even my teachers did not like it or encourage me to follow my dream." But, she says, her late father did encourage her and always encouraged her to do whatever she most wanted. But not so much her mother, says Glory, basically because she was retiring and did not condone her daughter's boldness.

Partly because of that, but also because the family home was being built – "we were five children in one bed" – while still at school she moved to live with her more supportive grandmother. "She was a lioness," remembers Glory. "She always did things differently."

The schoolgirl was one of only three selected from her primary school to attend secondary school, which she completed in 2008.

She managed to complete her secondary schooling but, because she did not earn a university pass, her father was greatly disappointed. This drove her to move away and to live with friends while starting the arduous task of finding a first job.

"But I was small and skinny," she says, "and struggled to find work." Then, as a young woman out in the world will, she fell in love. But the young man broke her heart and left her, jobless and pregnant. "But I don't blame him," she says generously. "We were not old enough and I believe our lives would be full of regrets if we had stayed together. My son carries his name and I wish him well."

Four years after finishing school she found work as a porter on the Kilimanjaro trekking circuit. "I've never seen a hard job like this in my life," she recalls, "so I respect all porters out there." On her first ascent she hit, as the sports saying goes, a brick wall and had to offer to pay a fellow porter to help carry her load. She had reached Barafu (ice) Camp at 468 metres and found herself knee-deep in snow and succumbing to hypothermia and possibly worse. She glissaded (skied on her backside) down wearing a black plastic bag for warmth. But that also caused her to sweat so she ended up colder than before.

But that, she later discovered, wasn't the worst of it. On your first climb as a porter you are not paid, but expected to live off the tips. However, because she spoke good English she bonded with some of the trekkers and so was able to pay the rent. Not all are so fortunate. "Now I remember all my guests," she maintains. "They are the reason I keep doing Kili. Small acts of kindness are what change the world."

But portering on Kilimanjaro is a back-breaking job, so Glory decided it was time to get licensed as a mountain guide instead and which, owing to a good school pass, she managed ... only to find that once again, on your first climb as a guide you are paid at only porter rates.

On that first trip she had to carry her own gear, extra water as well as a 12-kilogram emergency oxygen cylinder. On the way to the summit one of the clients suffered altitude sickness and Glory was assigned to add his load to her own while helping him to descend in the darkness. "I will always remember that night, it was very tough. I never wish that to happen again."

On reaching the office at base of the mountain she was given her mere porter's pay – but no tips, the financial lifeline of all guides and porters there. She was told the senior (male) guides had shared the pot among themselves and if she raised a fuss she would lose her job.

Lucky for her, at just that time, she heard of a tour company that was looking for women guides for an all-female trekking party, so off she went. That went so well she stayed with that same company for two years. But, she says with some regret, she found that, as a woman, things were tough. When she says "the men here see us a housewives", the implication is (and this was confirmed for me by a well established tour operator) that women guides and porters are sexually harassed and sometimes abused.

The other issue is that they have to leave families behind, including children, in a society where virtually all domestic work falls on them. They therefore have to rely heavily of relatives to fill in for them at home. On the other hand, they are able to bring home the ugali and nyama choli (the basic Tanzanian diet of stiff maize porridge and grilled meat).

Even though Glory was doing well professionally as a mountain guide, that also proved have its downside. "Most guests feel comfortable with us because we are good at TLC and as a result we get lots of tips and gifts and other faviours." But that only made her guide brother angry, so she decided to try out as a safari guide instead. Different job, SOS: being disdained by her peers as a woman guide in the bush.

It was that final straw that drove her to form her own company of all-women guide and porters back in Arusha, the base for Kilimanjaro trekking. The name she chose to register her business was Wilderness with Women. The Swahili equivalent is Porini na Mwanamke, but when she did internet searches under that name she found herself looking at "bad pictures".

A quick name change was needed, and the business has since grown markedly. One American client has proved to a steady supporter and patron, to date having sponsored the training of 20 others in the company, which now numbers 26 working in the not-for-profit Adventure Women Africa guiding operation.

It might seem like double-dealing to begin the final part of this chapter with a man, but it is what it is. Let's think of him as the starter for a braai: you don't give it much mind when you are tucking into a plate of juicy grilled fare. For our purposes we'll call him the Firelighter.

We pick up his story when he leaves his post as a special-ops agent in the Middle East. After that he went walkabout, and found his passion in wildlife conservation in Southern Africa, working with various rhino and elephant anti-poaching units – with great success in their various necks of the bushveld.

But, sensing he was trying to plug a leaking roof with fingers and thumbs, he sought his own place where he could make a real difference – the man had a vision. He remembered an old African idiom: if you educate a man you educate a person, but if you educate a woman you educate an entire village. What about an entire region, or a nation?

The thing is, in much of rural Africa, women have little status and are regarded as workers and sexual objects; sometimes the concept of rape hardly registers as a crime. Often while researching this chapter that word – rape – was a recurring theme. To break free from this virtual slavery appears to be a dream of every young woman in rural Africa. So, to begin, Firelighter needed to find a place in order to set his own dream into motion.

He found it at an old hunting block abutting Mana Pools National Park, which had been upended in 2014 by a ban in the USA on importing elephant trophies from Zimbabwe. The hunters moved out and poachers moved in to take aim at the valley's estimated 11 000 herd.

In an area with almost zero opportunities for outside employment, Firelighter sent out word to the local headman that he was looking to train women between ages of 18 and 35 for a special project. On the appointed day some 90 women arrived at Phundundu. Invariably, when questioned they related stories of domestic violence, sexual abuse, single mothers abandoned, Aids orphans … when you unpicked their stories they were all in some way victims of misogyny.

You can imagine that almost immediately everyone with an internet connection waded in with an opinion: they won't be up to it, you cannot arm women and send them out on bush patrols, you're nuts. Loudest of all, as you might imagine, were local men who insisted this was a job only a man could do. But Mr Blitz knew better.

He knew, for example, that the first women had recently graduated from the US Army's elite Ranger School, and that women routinely served in the combat units of various countries. He was also aware of women working as game or wildlife rangers in many other countries around the world. So why shouldn't they be trained as rangers to serve at the front line of the poaching war in Africa?

There was also a much sweeter incentive he could think of for his project. The supply of dollars for wildlife conservation was being spread increasingly thin. However, international funding for anything that helped to empower women, the poorer the better, was a much deeper reservoir from which to draw.

The Lower Zambezi's Colonel Kurtz assembled a team of instructors, all with extensive combat experience. Starting in mid-2017 they put their new recruits through a rigorous boot-camp routine, modelled on other special forces' selection regimens. Of the 37 women chosen to progress to the next phase, only three dropped out after being subjected to the "four pillars of misery": being kept hungry, cold, wet and tired for a prolonged period.

It was an astonishing success rate, given that most special forces expect a majority of (men) recruits to drop out within the first few phases of selection. When the Zambezi instructors took their charges on survival training they found the women often knew more than they did. They had so much more to gain, and so much more to lose, someone who observed the process commented.

After nearly three years operating in the park there has been a noticeable return of wildlife, they say. Also in that time the rangers, who call themselves Akashinga, the brave ones, have apprehended more than 70 poachers without having to fire a single shot. The top man realises that at some stage his bush soldiers will almost certainly get caught in a real firefight, but he's confident they'll handle it as well as any trained force possibly could.

Their secret? While men will tend to go into a contact situation with guns blazing, the Akashinga Rangers attempt always to de-escalate the situation. According to one of the training staff, this approach could usher in a new style of front-line conservation that relies more on education, empathy and getting community buy-in, than any other current implementation. When the Akashinga Rangers visit local villages, they are thronged like celebrities.

Since launching at Phundundu, Firelighter's vision has grown. He now envisages a corps of several thousand female rangers guarding buffer wildlife zones throughout Southern and East Africa, and why not? A filmmaker who documented the project commented on the change in the women's demeanour. In material terms they are flying as well, able to achieve what previously was too dangerous to dream. Things like getting a driver's licence, buying property, completing their educations and that of their children. As one of the rangers told a visiting journalist: "When you employ men they can be irresponsible with money, despite the fact that they have kids. But with women, once they get money, in most cases they support their kids."

It feels like the toughest job in Africa has been invigorated with the fire of passion bearing a compassionate face.

Animal Intelligence: Stand Back, We're Not Sure How Deep This Thing Goes

JUST WHAT IS THIS INTELLIGENCE thing anyway? It seems like such a simple question, that should have an equally straightforward answer, but the more you delve into what it means the further down a darkening tunnel you'll find yourself falling. For millennia, sage people have turned this philosopher's stone over and over and come up with, not exactly naught, but not so much as we might hope.

For much of those millennia it was presumed that only humans possessed real intelligence, and souls to add. But more and more this picture of things is fading into a dramatisation of *Homo sapiens*' self-importance. Surely whatever can feel pain, hunger or thirst needs to be considered a living, feeling thing worthy of, if not empathy, then at least sympathy?

Anyone who has ever known, better still worked with, what are known as super herding dogs, the likes of collies, kelpies and heelers, will know language is no barrier to communication with them. They'll pick up the rules through the slightest of signals with very little other instruction required, sometimes just a small hand motion repeated once, much less than most humans would need. Animal psychologists have worked out that most dogs can learn up to 165 spoken words and respond as expected. With the super herders that number goes up to as many as 250.

Just watch a squall-seasoned shepherd with his or her sheep dog to see poetry in motion, the mystery of survival turned work to play. Then again, these dogs are born with the instincts to herd just about anything and their amazing adeptness is, after all, an extension of hunting and killing.

I once had a much-loved border collie who, from when she was a puppy, would learn new tricks in just one lesson. There was a more famous one named Chaser who could recognise a thousand objects by their names. But as self-described animal communicator Anna Breytenbach insists, using proficiency in a human language as an indicator of animal intelligence falls way short of a valid test. It's like using proficiency in English as an indication of a non-speaker's IQ.

Some organisations involved in game-guide training have realised that even literacy is no measure of bush smarts or intelligence wholesale. Which is why the likes of the Zimbabwean Professional Hunters and Guides Association (ZPGA) and the Field Guides Association of Southern Africa (FGASA) allow all exams to be taken orally.

I know of people who would side with Jonathan Swift when he put horses in charge in the Land of the Houyhnhmns, to rule over the brutish Yahoos, the humans. Even Roman emperor Caligula tried to make his favourite horse, Incitatus, a senator. But then the emperor was crackers, and anyway he was assassinated before he could pull it off.

But the point still holds, that there are people who prefer horses to other humans. Horses are just so aloof and mostly hard to get close to (kind of equine cats you might say). They seem to exude a deeper understanding than we generally allow them. And yet these are the same creatures that will carry us unflinching till they drop, or into the maw of cannon fire.

Anyone who has worked closely with horses or dogs, gorillas or chimpanzees, elephants or whales, will vouch that not only do their charges possess deep intelligence (albeit of a slightly different kind to ours), but souls too. Often spirits much more noble than the Yahoos who think they are in control. If you consider life over the long term, humans have made a right real hash of the place we call home. Other animals not so much: so who's starting to look like the smart ones now?

It has long been fashionable in the community of animal behavioural science to avoid, at all costs, anthropomorphising animals (bestowing on them any human trait, such as higher intelligence or feelings). However, there is a growing body of research, as well as accumulated observations in the field, which suggests that in denying animals any smarts, the humanists have really been living in a world of zoomorphism.

We're a narcissistic bunch that was recently gifted its very own personal mirror pool: the selfie-enabled mobile phone. For the most part this has had us viewing any and all other species as inferior, non-sentient, devoid of souls, spirits, feelings: just look what we do to farm animals, keeping them in conditions akin to slave ships of old, denying them any feelings at all!

The 19th-century oft-named founding father of environmentalism John Muir noted: "In nothing does man, with his grand notions of heaven and charity, show forth his innate, low-bred, wild animalism more clearly than in his treatment of his brother beasts."[16] Numerous more recent thinkers and writers, including Jared Diamond and Yuval Noah Harari, have said much the same.

The late great naturalist and author Henry Beston put it even more succinctly: "The animal shall not be measured by man. In a world older and more complete than ours, they move finished and complete, gifted with extension of the senses we have lost or never attained, living by voices we shall never hear."[17]

Circuses and caged animals have for millennia thrilled humans with how clever some of them seem to be, without us really thinking much more deeply about it. But how do parrots learn to not only mimic human speech but also have a sense of the meaning – not to mention a sense of humour? How else could their comic timing be so stupendous? It's not only parrots that are great mimics, but also crows, mynahs, robins and drongos, which are all first-class impersonators.

---

[16] John Muir, *The Complete Works: Travel Memoires, Wilderness Essays, Environmental Studies & Letters,* Chapter XII, "Zigzags Among the Polar Pack", Delphi Classics, 2017.

[17] Henry Beston, *The Outermost House,* Doubleday and Doran, first edition 1928; subsequently Henry Holt & Co, New York

Lyrebirds can imitate up to 20 other bird species in the forests where they live in Australia, as well as car alarms, cameras with motor drives and chain saws.

On the Isle of Coll in the Scottish Inner Hebrides, there is a family of common starlings that has lived on a ledge in an old bothie (shelter) uninhabited by humans for several decades. Throughout that time the old bothie's generator has lain in disrepair, meanwhile at least four generations of starlings have come and gone. And yet today when that family sings, incorporated into their song you'll hear the unmistakable sound of a two-stroke engine firing up, spluttering to life and then running for several seconds.

What about animal feelings? What do we say about a mother baboon who carries its dead baby around for weeks; or a killer whale observed to have pushed its dead calf around the water for 17 days; or elephants that stay with their dead calves when the herd has pushed off?

After horses and dogs, animal trainers and behaviouralists began to tell us that dolphins and whales, gorillas and chimpanzees had much richer social lives than we'd previously given them credit for. This included the entire gambit of "human" characteristics that just decades before was still being taught as the things that set us apart from them.

In more recent times the intersection of observation and knowledge between indigenous people, dedicated animal researchers, game rangers and tour guides in the bush has resulted in a much broader, as well as deeper, understanding of wild creatures than was previously evident. We've seen videos of hippos saving antelope from crocodile attacks, a hippo in a waterhole in Hwange pushing around a water pipe and then a large crocodile as though it was a pool toy, and the rhino and hippo "date night".

Animal behaviouralists in general don't like the idea of any kind of altruism out there because, in the big picture of evolutionary theory, it is a situation that aids the receiver at the expense of the giver, diminishing their chances of survival. However, the giver need not lose anything in sharing, or helping those of other species. I can add an example of what is arguably the most intriguing that we know of to date. On Mombo Island in the Okavango Delta back in 2013, a lone female wild dog, which the local guides named Solo, seemed to be spending an inordinate amount of time hanging with different pairs of black-backed jackals.

When one of the pairs had pups, Solo adopted them as her own pack and helped the jackals to rear the pups. But things soured between the adult animals as they competed over childcare until the jackal parents moved their pups to a new den (something not noted previously). That was when events took an even stranger turn with the female wild dog kidnapping three of the four jackal offspring.

There followed days of recapture by the jackals, re-kidnapping by the wild dog, until a truce was reached. After that Solo and the adult jackals would even go off hunting together (the wild dog slowing down for her short-legged accomplices to keep up). How this played out in the end was not recorded, but it makes you think that there is more going on out there than even good old Horatio could figure.

Just what is this brainpower thing anyway? I remember my first year in journalism school, when we were taught that complex communication was the thing that set us apart from all other species: today that notion would be laughed out of the lecture room. Even bees know better than that.

People who study "low" forms of life such as lichens, algae and fungi find they have apparatuses that work not entirely unlike our central nervous systems. Take mycelium for example, those networks of fine hyphae, sticky fibres of fungi that bind soil and intertwine with plant roots in a mutually beneficial existence of resource sharing.

It's been called the "wood wide web" and it's been discovered that hyphae comprise hollow fibres that convey messages via hydraulic, chemical and even electrical pulses. The way they work is not unlike the human brain. Not exactly like, but close enough to lead us to ask: are these living, thinking things? In truth how they work is less intuitive than humans and more binary (on or off) like the way computers work and the basis of artificial intelligence.

Anyone who has spent time hunting mosquitoes in the dark recesses of the bedroom at night might agree with me that, pound for pound, or milligram for milligram in their case, these fragile-bodied critters have serious acumen and wiles. They weigh on average around five milligrams, and will all too often outwit you, weighing in at, on average, between 70 and 100 million milligrams. Go figure, as they say.

I'M NO EXPERT IN ANTHROPOLOGY or animal behaviour, but I have spent some time among animals and have seen some strange things out there in the noösphere.[18] I recall while rambling around the Magaliesberg, sitting on a ridge and watching a pair of black eagles swooping and soaring, playing the uplift as well as with each other. I would swear it was play. Do birds have a sense of fun or was this just my own soppy, unscientific anthropomorphising? It's hard to say for sure, but so exuberant was the display there was no more fitting explanation.

I was fortunate, some years later, to live in close proximity to elephants and watch their behaviour. Talk about smart: they were – at least some of them – positively devious. A marula tree shaded our camp's bush kitchen and while it was in fruit elephants would arrive en masse each morning to feed, causing havoc with our breakfast service. The staff got smart and early one morning, before the sweet-toothed animals arrived, they gathered all the fallen fruits onto a canvas sheet and threw them in the veld some way off.

When the animals duly arrived and did not find their amuse-bouche, they trashed the tree and the kitchen tent. Every other day I was lured into a game of hide-and-seek as they sought to steal food from our store or raid our garden plants. Funny thing was – and it was invariably lone bulls – each one was quite different and I had to be careful to use appropriate tactics to see them off. One wrong move and I could be in big trouble.

I would chase them off with general success, excepting in the case of one big bull we dubbed Grumpy Gus who was unusually unpredictable and aggressive (when he died a necropsy found a nasty abscess on the root of one tusk). Something I quickly found with the

---

[18] The noösphere is a recent theoretical construct, describing the envelope of consciousness that envelopes the Earth, much like the atmosphere of the biosphere.

others was that they all seemed to know and respect exactly where my territory ended and, if I crossed the line, they would turn and charge. Jump back over the line and they'd back off.

We intuit that large animals like whales and elephants will be smart due to having large brains in their large bodies. This is partly true, but brain size alone is not a measure of absolute intelligence (whatever that might be). Brain size relative to body size seems to count for more. Neanderthals had larger brains than we "sentient apes" but we got the better of them in the end.

Sperm whales have the largest brains of any creature. We don't have much data on them, but if we use song repertoire as some measure of intelligence they are up there. Leeches on the other hand have 32 tiny brains, and octopuses nine somewhat bigger ones, so who can really say what's going on out there in the noösphere?

Some evolutionary psychologists reckon large brains and complex intellects arose from the need to navigate complex social networks. Merlin Sheldrake,[19] who studies mushrooms and their mycelial root systems, says that even the smallest of interactions are entangled with shifting social networks. If it applies to fungi, then how much more so to dolphins, apes, whales or elephants? Each of these species lives within, and cannot survive without, large social groups and none more so than elephants.

Elephant ecologist Stephen Blake points out that the web of social entanglement for most people seldom extends beyond 200: family, school or work associates, sports partners, professionals and other friends. For an elephant that number is three to five times as many, and it has to remember each individual or face physical confrontation and even rejection.

Elephants' fabulous, famous memories also have to remember where to find food over vast ranges, what the dangers will be on crossing big rivers, and what to expect on the other side. People who work and live in such areas notice that elephants are extremely alert when crossing from safe to unsafe areas and their conduct changes correspondingly.

---

[19] Merlin Sheldrake, *Entangled Life: How Fungi Make Our Worlds, Change Our Minds and Shape Our Futures,* The Bodley Head, London, 2020.

When looking at brain size, an elephant's averages 5 kilograms, the largest of any land animal as you would expect. And, while the bigger whales have much larger ones – between two and four times so – their bodies are as much as 20 times larger. Aristotle described elephants as the animals that "surpass all others in wit and mind". He would have been familiar with the great pachyderms as various armies used them at the time, including that of his favourite student Alexander, later dubbed The Great.

Not surprisingly elephants have an exceptionally large hippocampus – the part of the brain dedicated to memory. It's been suggested that, due to their similarly large cerebral cortex, the part of the brain used for cognitive processing, we should place them alongside great apes when it comes to bush smarts.

As well as manifesting behaviours including mimicry, compassion, a wide range of communication and play, researchers have noted they even show self-recognition – supposedly a sign of deep awareness that increasingly is being conferred on great apes and marine mammals. However, when it comes to brain size and memory, squirrels have to be sitting near the top of that tree. Come winter they can find more than 100 locations where they've stashed nuts during the summer. Most of us would struggle to find just one. Where are my car keys!?

ABOUT THE MOST INTERESTING THING we have learned about humpback whales – ever since we found out they sang, back in the 1960s when American biologist Roger Payne dragged a hydrophone behind his yacht and heard male humpback whales belting out "exuberant, uninterrupted rivers of sound" – is that they are quite literally hip-hop crazy about music.

When their vocalisations are unpacked it turns out they create songs that can last up to 30 minutes, using rhyme and rhythm, phrasing and melodies, much like we do when composing music. During mating season singing sessions have been heard to last as long as 22 hours. Five species are known to sing: blue, bowhead, fin, humpback and minke, although the two largest – blue and fin, the bass singers in the cetacean chorus – mostly sing at pitches below human hearing.

But that is hardly the most interesting thing about them. University of St Andrews (UK) whale researcher Ellen Garland analysed humpback whale songs across the wide sweep of the South Pacific Ocean over a number of years. She found songs spread from region to region. While clans of whales tended to sing from their own song sheets, new repertoires seemed to originate off the coast of Australia. By the time they reached French Polynesia they had been modified much like a pop song that is covered over and over again.

Garland found that, whenever a new song appeared in an area, it would replace older ones like an ongoing top-of-the-pops playlist. "When a whale hits open-mic night with a hot new number, locals drop their old ballads and belt out a new one," writes *National Geographic* staff writer Craig Welch.[20]

Sperm whales use their enormous brains (up to 20 kilograms) to operate nature's largest inborn sonar system. Essentially it is used for locating squid prey in the dark ocean depths, but clearly it has developed into something more than just that. Hal Whitehead, biology professor at Dalhousie University in Nova Scotia, discovered their clicks were actually part of an elaborate language. Also, that there were regional dialects as different as the English spoken in the Scottish Highlands is from that in Jamaica. Different whale clans also exhibited quite different behavioural habits.

Sperm whale specialist Shane Gero believes his subjects have clan "surnames" as well as individual names, which are used in sub-visual communications to tell others who is down there hunting giant squid, or just hanging around (when sleeping they hang suspended in mid-water for up to two hours at a time). Gero has even identified non-specific sperm whale "baby talk" before they learn the clan code. Does this all equate to whale culture, or cultures, poses Welch? Not all marine scientists think so, but increasingly more do.

When we look more deeply into the tidal pool of species self-absorption, we'll be shocked to find that one of the things reflecting back at us is a worm that's been down there for nigh on 600 million years.

---

[20] "Secrets of the Whales", *National Geographic,* May 2021.

The Octopus, a Wiggly Worm and Us

We humans have created a number of hierarchies that aim to put ourselves at the acme of each, including The Bible, the food chain, and even Charles Darwin's "tree of life"; although that has been misconstrued. If you think you are at the pinnacle of, say, the food chain, just go and swim among a shoal of great white sharks and then see how peak you feel about that. We even create zoomorphic gods like centaurs and minotaurs to show who's who in the zoo.

As mentioned in the previous chapter, people who investigate animal intelligence, plant intelligence and even that of organisms that occupy branches on the tree of life below that of plants, such as fungi, are increasingly reporting from the noösphere back to Mothership that they too have not only feelings, and comprehensions, and intelligence, but even – perhaps – consciousness and self-awareness.

In the three domains of life – archae (the really oldest, smallest stuff, most of which can live in extremely hostile environments); bacteria (similar to archae, but a bit more advanced in their molecular make-up and abilities); and eukaryotes (protozoa, fungi, chromista, stuff like algae and diatoms, then plants and animals, including us) – the deeper we delve the more we tumble into a vortex of complexity. It's the old William Blake thing of seeing worlds in grains of sand, or galaxies in single cells.

So back to horses and dogs, gorillas and chimps, elephants and whales – but now also considering cephalopods (octopuses, nautiluses and squid). When looking back down the tree of life to see where we come from, past monkeys, birds and fish, we find we last shared a common ancestor with cephalopods around 600 million years ago (mya). It was a simple marine flat worm with two light-sensitive spots, one on each side of its body.

This worm-thing swam or more likely kind of undulated about (much like the nudibranchs that inhabit coral reefs today) in some shallow Ediacaran sea. That's where the Ediacara Hills in the outback of South Australia now stand and where its fossil was first found; whence the Ediacaran Era.

Those light receptors suggest some very important anatomical advances from the slime moulds, algae and bacteria that had previously dominated life on Earth (although at that time, until around 350 mya, it was all in the sea). First, it had to have some kind of simple nervous system for processing the incoming light information, and second, a bilateral body design that we share with all our ancestors from that point onwards.

That major split 600 mya marks one of the great divides of the two principle branches of animal life: vertebrate and invertebrate. For the sake of completion, the arthropods, including insects, ants, lobsters and suchlike, branched off from the molluscan bough (on which are draped the multi-armed cephalopods that are the principle subject of this chapter) some time later.

There are around 300 species of cephalopod, ranging from about 2 centimetres to 7 metres in span. On the long road from the Ediacaran to now, among those that disappeared along the way include a giant cuttlefish-type creature with a 3-metre-long spiral shell that was the scourge of the oceans back when.

Talking shells, modern cephalopods are essentially molluscs, in the class of shellfish, but ones that discarded their shells between 160 and 200 mya. It was this turn of events that is thought to have led to the sudden – relatively speaking – development of complex brains that were necessary to survive the relentless predation on the reefs on which most of them live. The journey from simple worm to modern octopus was just as convoluted as was ours.

What we see here is the almost incomprehensible reality of evolution building two of its most intricate systems not once, but twice, along completely different roads: the complex brain and the camera eye (as opposed to the compound one that all other arthropods have). Cephalopods swim as "an island of mental complexity in a sea of invertebrate animals," says philosopher of science and evolutionary theory, Peter Godfrey-Smith.[21]

The cephalopod brain is very different to ours, as we shall see in time, but one thing it does is completely debunk the notion of mammalian mental superiority. One thing – usually both the first and the last – we notice about an octopus is that it can change shape and colour in the blink of an eye. They are the ultimate shape shifters and for all the world have no fixed shape at all.

Their bodies are covered with nodes, called papillae, that can have them resembling a smooth balloon one moment, a spiky coral reef the next, a hook or a lance. The only solid parts of its body are its eyeballs and beak, so it can fit through a hole only slightly larger than its eye. Disappearing comes naturally to them. It's no wonder its Afrikaans name is seekat – sea cat.

Early experiments with octopuses, in the mid-20th century, tended to be barbaric (basically pulling off bits to see how they reacted) and simplistically contrived, so few headline-grabbing discoveries were made. Also, from a theoretical perspective that approach was very plodding: more about "what" than "how" or "why". Much of it was repeating the kind of "lever pulling for food" ploys used at the time to test various animal abilities in laboratories.

But things change and in the intervening years scientific methodology got a whole lot more sophisticated and enlightened. The first major realisation, with both octopuses and most other animals, was that members of any species were not all the same; they were much more interesting than that. In marine laboratories it was found some octopuses liked or disliked different humans. Ones they disliked they might squirt with jets of water: in one case, for no discernible reason, it was especially personal and sustained.

Octopuses can be surprisingly funny and are also exceptional escape artists. There are numerous marine-lab rumours about octopuses in tanks stealing out at night and climbing into adjacent

---

[21] Peter Godfrey-Smith, *Other Minds: The Octopus and the Evolution of Intelligent Life,* William Collins/Harper Collins, London 2017.

tanks to enjoy seafood buffets, then returning before daylight to stare all balefully out of their glass prison cells.

The stories were finally verified by CCTV cameras at the National Aquarium of New Zealand. An octopus the researchers there named Inky was seen squeezing through a narrow gap at the top of its tank, slithering across the floor and making a dash for freedom. He (or possibly she) found a drainage pipe and took the 15-centimetre gap. Luckily for Inky it lead directly to the sea and he or she was gone.

These octo-creatures can also be playful and highly inquisitive. One marine facility discovered this (to its detriment) when aquarium staff arrived one morning and found their very expensive flooring inundated with 750 litres of salt water. The occupant of one tank had taken apart a water outflow valve with the result that all the contents spilled out. Another was caught in the act jamming an arm down an outflow valve with the same effect. In another case an octopus would shoot jets of water at lights and cause them to short-circuit – repeatedly. Throw just about anything non-edible into its tank and it will almost certainly become the next water-polo projectile.

Maybe the most entertaining tale of octopus wit comes from Millersville University, Pennsylvania, marine biologist Jean Boal. She was feeding her subjects thawed squid which, she found out in good time, they did not like at all: what they liked most was crab or other fresh shellfish. After dropping off squid bits for her research subjects, when Boal walked back past one specific tank its occupant took a piece of old squid, waved it around and – while staring the human down – shoved it into the outlet valve. All told octopuses have proved to be rather dull as lever pullers, yet surprisingly proficient at DIY.

Godfrey-Smith defines the behaviour of octopuses in their natural habitats as "curious, flexible, adventurous and opportunistic". He recounts a case in Indonesia where they were seen using two different-sized half-coconut shells, carrying them around, looking for all the world like multi-legged trolleys. When danger approached they would quickly slide inside the smaller one while pulling the larger over to form a hard spherical shell. Gone in one second. You can just see it inside there, four arms up and four down, sucking firmly and creating a tight seal for its octosphere.

Some fun facts about the wondrous octopus:
- They have three hearts which pump blue-green blood. Their blood uses copper instead of iron, as does ours, to carry oxygen, giving it that unique hue.
- Less than half their brain power (neurons) is located in their head brains. Around two-thirds of their approximately 500 million neurons are located in the arms, each of which operates like an independent satellite brain.

The inspiring documentary *My Octopus Teacher* revealed something unexpected: most octopuses live little more than 18 months, few beyond 24. Even some mice live longer than that (between two and seven years). A bigger question is, why do we age at all, when our individual cells are being regularly replaced?

(The answer lies in the mechanics of evolution, with the selection and deselection of short- and long-term genetic "faults". This results in the individuals of a species having a high likelihood for either an early or a late death. Those with an early likelihood, compounded over time, breed themselves to extinction. That means that there are increasingly more of the ones with a late likelihood of dying to inherit the Earth. But we need to be talking about octopuses here, so back to the present.)

It appears that octopuses live for only one reproductive cycle, the female tending the egg broods and all the while not eating. Once the eggs hatch the adult begins to fade in both colour and condition and eventually falls to pieces, or is torn apart by predators. Why these soft-bodied molluscs should have such short lifespans seems to be a consequence of giving up their shells and having to live extremely high-energy lives surviving in the highly dangerous world of shallow, warm-water environments.

There is one known exception and that is the Californian deep-water octopus, *Graneledone boreopacifica*. Using an ROV at depths down to 3000 metres, scientists at a Monterey marine laboratory watched a female tend her brood for four-and-a-half years before they hatched, and then she literally fell apart. It is thought this species might live for up to 16 years. Why? Because the near-freezing temperatures where they live greatly slow down their life processes, while the extreme depth significantly lessens the pressures of predation.

And then there's that cephalopod skin. They have three distinct layers, each with different light-producing capabilities. Basically octopuses, and even more so large cuttlefish, are swimming LED display boards, with 10-megapixel screens controlled by the central head brain – in part. The outermost layer has cells called chromatophores, colour sacks like ink-filled balloons that are surrounded by radial muscles which can make them expand or contract. These produce the reds and yellows.

The next layer has reflecting cells called iridophores that can split incoming wavelengths of light and project back the shimmering, metallic mainly blues and greens. Finally, there is the bottom-most leucophore layer, which scholars of Greek will gather is responsible for the pale colour range. This is done by pure reflection of ambient "white" light.

But it is the combination of all three that gives them such startling and variable colour options. Sometimes the colours reflect moods, sometimes aggressive postures, sometimes straightforward camouflage (which of course is far from simple), sometimes what seems to be a meditative resting pattern characterised by "clouds" of dark and light moving across the body. Also observed are colour "explosions" without any apparent cause. Maybe mood.

What is most startling is that these animals seem to be colour-blind: so how do they do this, especially perfectly matching intricate backgrounds the like of coral reefs when in camouflage mode? Remember those satellite brains? It appears the skin of the arms can see. The how of it is not understood much beyond that, though.

With startling colour-matching, combined with an almost infinite capacity for body morphing, an octopus can flick between coral reef, rock, piece of kelp or sandy bottom in mere milliseconds (200 to be a bit more exact). That's not so sluggish for a spineless, shell-less shellfish.

Seldom Seen at the Place of New Beginnings

THEY ARE SELDOM SEEN YET they can be found almost everywhere on our planet where there is plant material and water available – they being termites. Although they form a completely different animal group from ants, the study of both is referred to as myremecology even though, technically, it means the study of ants.

Anyone who studied savanna ecology will almost certainly have learned that their total biomass exceeds by far that of all its mammals. Termites are exclusively detritivores and eat mostly dead plant material, including the faeces of herbivores. It's been estimated that in the savanna biome they process up to 90 per cent of all dry plant matter, mostly tall grasses and trees.

The problem, for them, is that tall grasses and trees are comprised largely of cellulose, a long, honeycomb "polysaccharide" molecule (the most abundant organic polymer on the planet). It forms the walls of plant cells and gives them their rigidity, which also makes it very hard – in most cases impossible – for animals, both them and us, to digest: it's often the "fibre" part in health foods. Grass is relatively soft and it can be digested by the group called microtermes. In their guts they have a nice relationship with a host of microbes that break down the cellulose internally.

Relative to wood that is. Dealing with dead timber is the job of a group called the macrotermes, which have had to become farmers in order to feed themselves. The specific branch of agriculture they practice is called fungiculture: they grow fungal gardens deep in the bowels – almost quite literally[22] – of their termiteria, to which they feed partially digested wood fibre.

It is the job of the fungi to break it down further into a kind of mushroomy blancmange on which the fat, white, wood-gathering termes can then feast. (I lie awake at night wondering about things like: do they chew on the natural occurring layers of calcrete limestone that are prevalent in our region to deal with heartburn? You never know, it's a weird and wicked world out there.)

The specific kind of fungus tended by the wood eaters is called Termitomyces and it must be kept permanently moist and warm. Therefore, wherever you see a termite mound you know they will have hit ground water, as deep in 30 metres if needs be. The above-ground towers we see are really elaborate air-conditioning systems that have been measured as tall as 14 metres. The interior temperature must be kept at a constant, approximately 30°C, depending on the species, so tunnels inside are opened and closed to direct the flow of hot and cool air inside.

The mounds are composed of soil mixed with termite saliva that renders it into a cement-hard clay. Africans know the material as "dagha" and historically it has been used extensively in the construction of homes – as well as all-weather tennis courts. I'm not sure about the longevity of the tennis courts but the ruined remains of some dagha structures date back several centuries.

In the dark hours I also mull over stuff like, just how many termites are there, and how many mammals would that equate to? I went digging on my own and discovered some other insomniac had done the hard work. He or she has estimated that there are a bewildering 10 000 trillion ants working hard on Earth to recycle all the dead plant matter. I subjected this little nugget of data to some creative bookkeeping, starting with the assumption that the number refers to both true ants and white ants, otherwise termites.

The next assumption was that they would be distributed evenly

---

[22] It was South African polymath Eugene Marais who first postulated that a termite colony could be likened to a single living organism with its own brain, circulatory and immune system, and the digestive system we are discussing here.

across six continents. Then I weighed a million termites and found their average mass to be 1 milligram (just kidding, I Googled that). Then it was assumed that half (mostly the ants) live in forests and the other half in grass-woodland mosaics, aka savanna, which are our guys.

For the benefit of aspiring myrmecologists, ants and termites are not at all closely related: termites are close cousins of cockroaches (especially wood-eating cockroaches of the genus Cryptocercus), while ants are more closely allied to wasps.

Anyway, I crunched the numbers and came up with a biomass of …. 800 billion kilograms of little crawlers scurrying around under and over our sub-Saharan veld. With an estimated average mass of 50 kilograms for mammals (which is generous given that most of them are bats), it would equate to a population of 16 billion mammals living in the African savanna, and just imagine that!

Out there on the endless African plains there are some 1 000 species of termites: just one, the southern harvester *Hodotermes mossabicus* (admittedly among the most widespread and numerous), has been found in the stomachs of 65 species of birds (including farm chickens), 19 mammals as well as various lizards, blind or worm snakes, frogs, a large variety of insects (beetles, wasps, assassin bugs, cockroaches, centipedes, dragonflies) as well as their associates spiders and scorpions.

But of all these, it is ants that are the main enemy of soft-bodied termites and great battles can be seen being waged between them when an army of raider ants attacks a termite colony. The drama and trauma that ensues equal anything from the sagas of the Iliad, Genghis Khan or Mzilikazi.

What kid has not been enthralled coming across a column of harvester termite workers (exclusively females in case you wondered) in the veld, carrying off half the bushveld like looters at a shopping mall in downtown Joburg? A column out in the open will enjoy the protection of soldier sentries, but you might also have seen the covered runways along the ground or up the trunk of a dead tree.

Much more entertaining is coming across a phalanx of army ants on the rampage. Our Matabele ants, *Megaponera analis*, are among the largest ant species in the world and they feed exclusively on termites. Their common name tells us all we need to know about their feeding behaviour, derived from the fierce warriors of King Mzilikazi who terrorised the region when raiding was all the rage during the Mfecane[23] insurrection.

Most raids occur in the early morning and evening. The action begins with ant scouts moving out to locate a likely target, taking care not to make contact, and then beetling back to their nest while laying a pheromone trail as they go. Once home, they spend between one and five minutes recruiting raiders. When a raiding party has assembled they move out en masse and in file, all castes taking part – soldiers, minor workers and major workers.

On approaching the termite mound they stop a way off, gather around the leading scouts, then fan out to encircle the target. The major workers then set to breaking up the outer protective skin of the termitarium. Wherever it is breached the minors rush in and dispatch termites with a sting, then drag them outside to the congregating area. From there they return in formation, with the majors carrying the dead termites in their jaws.

A piece of amber recovered from the Salt River Mine in Chiapas State, Mexico, and dated to the Late Jurassic period (circa 160 mya), contains just such a scene frozen in time: three Aztec (*Azteca*) ants and three *Nasutitermes* termites, as well as a *Neivamyrmex* soldier ant with a *Nasutitermes* worker termite in its jaws.

THE TECHNICAL TERM FOR EATING ants is myrmecophagy, and haven't we all. This is often used to describe eating termites as well, whereas the more correct term for that is termitophagy. However, since most animals that eat the one kind are also partial to the other, we'll lump them together because the task of actually sorting and counting could lead to a deep kind of wretchedness.

---

[23] The Mfecane, also Difaqane, was a period spanning the 1800s when various tribes were caught in a vice between European expansionists pushing from the southwest and slave traders from the northeast. The resulting violence, and emergence of various warlords, displaced millions of people across Southern Africa.

Ornithologists quoted in the seventh edition of *Roberts* who studied the stomach contents of ostriches, using something they called the "cafeteria experiment", found the big birds much preferred just one species, another southern harvester termite *Microhodotermes viator* (the "viator" part telling us they like to fly). You do have to wonder how researchers can tell one species from another and sort from all the other mush in there.

The other 64 bird species of those referenced above include just about all the ones you might see feeding on the ground from bustards through owls, francolins, hornbills, storks, rollers, some bee-eaters, larks and pipits, scrub robins, chats (not least of all the ant-eating one) and even Egyptian geese. Then there are those that snatch the alates in the air, namely swifts and swallows – but also some bigger and unexpected ones.

Steppe and lesser-spotted eagles breed mainly across Central Asia and time their arrivals along the northerly edge of Southern Africa to coincide with the first summer rains. This is also when termites schedule their grand nuptial flights when we see them as flying ants. The first we notice these raptors is when they gather along a front stretching from the Okavango wetlands down the Zambezi valley in late October.

By early November they'll be moving into the South African Lowveld and the southern Kalahari, as if gliding on the storm front. In those areas you can see these brown eagles on the ground feasting in congregations of tens or even hundreds, stuffing themselves on termites that have done their love dance, shed their wings and begun looking for a suitable spot to start their own subterranean dynasties. Zap!

You might have surmised that ants make up a significant menu item on the African plains, along with termites, but it is much more likely to be the eggs than the adult ants which themselves can be distasteful to downright dangerous (see: Matabele ants above, and bullet ants, chapter 5). Some other harmless creatures have evolved fierce ant-lookalike disguises to fool would-be predators.

These mimics are called myremecomorphs and include among them quite a few kinds of small spiders (around 300 species), as well as some true bugs, crickets, stick insects, mantids, flies, beetles and thrips. Then there are the myremecophiles, those creatures that feed pretty much exclusively on ants, but since they tend to live elsewhere they are of no concern to us here.

Excepting for one, which will be of interest to those of us who grew up watching ants, and that is antlions. They are the larval stage of lacewings, the adults named for their large diaphanous pinions. Lacewings are harmless to anyone or anything other than the likes of aphids, whiteflies, caterpillars and various leaf-eating beetles and bugs, so it's little wonder gardeners welcome their presence as much as they do ladybugs.

While the adults look like charming but over-sized damselflies, their larvae are among the most ferocious looking of creatures we encounter underfoot or in our veld tool boxes. Most striking is their proportionately massive set of inward curving jaws. The formidable micro-predators dig inverted conical sand traps and lie just below the surface at the apex waiting for an ant to avalanche down the steep slope.

Kids can spend ages with pieces of grass learning how to imitate trapped ants, only to snatch up the lunging "little five". The Kalahari breeds hardened types and the kids there have to learn to do battle with the biggest ant lions in the world, some of which will span an adult's palm.

What just about all Southern African myremecophagists have in common is you'll find them in termite central, which happens to be the southern Kalahari. Some decades ago a young English businessman named Stephen Boler, having made a fortune by age 35 selling cut-price car tyres, exhaust pipes and kitchens, came on safari to the area and fell in love with it. (During his lifetime he was the main money behind Manchester City Football Club.)

He started buying up exhausted old cattle farms, eventually acquiring somewhat north of 100 000 hectares of red-duned arid savanna. He called his place "new beginning" or Tswalu in the local lingo. But it was not just about having his own private game reserve for the boasting rights and, along with the general game he re-introduced part of his vision for Tswalu was for the breeding of rare and endangered species such as roan and sable, cheetah and wild dog, although the Mancunian has long moved on to the great hunting ground.

Needless to say the business big wheel was just as smart when it came to planning his succession. It is written that, although he met Nicky Oppenheimer only once, he sensed a kindred spirit: in his will Boler bequeathed his Kalahari love child to the South African-born "gold lord" on the basis of first refusal. The founder of Tswalu died not many years later[24] and today it is the Oppenheimers who call the shots (among their first order of business was to discontinue the hunting that had been part of Boler's eco-tourism formula).

They also inherited a substantial biomass of termites as well as all the things that eat them. Thus, they are able to promote the "seldom-seen five" as a discerning marketing counter to the Big Five safari cliché. The group comprises aardvark, pangolin, aardwolf, brown hyena and bat-eared fox – but can you pick the odd one out from the line-up?

Some wannabe game rangers will call out "bat-eared fox" on the basis that they are not at all rare in the Kalahari, in fact quite the contrary. Others might say brown hyena, and I would side with them, on the basis that they do not eat termites other than in the most opportunistic manner, like when you dab at crumbs on a breadboard while eating a sandwich and pick up a few, well, ants maybe.

For the sake of numerical harmony the hyena could be replaced by the Cape fox (*Vulpes chama*), the only true fox of sub-Saharan Africa and a near Southern African endemic: the distribution just edges north into south-eastern Angola. Although their population is considered to be stable, they are nevertheless extremely shy creatures and a lifer for many bush connoisseurs.

Although classed as small predators on account of their being able to take the likes of hares and game birds, the larger part of their diet consists of burrowing insects and their larvae, and termites (primarily the harvester species *Hodotermes mossambicus*). In spite of this intelligence, stock farmers persecute them across their range. But not nearly as much as they do aardwolves which are extremely

---

[24] In a car crash en route to Tswalu, if this is of any interest.

rare, secretive and eat almost entirely termites and insect larvae. They do, though, have the unfortunate fate of looking quite like their more wolfish hyena relatives.

All good and well, but it's hard to entice people into the Kalahari with the promise of foxes and ant-wolves any more than antlions. It's aardvarks and pangolins that are the star performers on the "seldom seen" safari checklist. Especially pangolins, which have become the poster species for wildlife conservation worldwide.

Collectively the eight species of pangolins are believed to be the world's most targeted animals by the illegal wildlife trade: the IUCN Red Data List classifies three species as critically endangered, another three as endangered and two (including our own *Smutsia temminckii*) as vulnerable.

Our local species used to be known as *Manis temminckii* but changed quite recently. You might think the renaming honoured former Renaissance man JC Smuts, but you'd be wrong. It was an otherwise little remembered person back in 1832 who collected the first one for scientific benefit. Temminck, though, is famous for having a slew of creatures named after him (20 birds, 14 mammals, 10 fishes, two reptiles and a shark).

That happens when you are a Dutch aristocrat and some of your family are high movers in the Dutch East India Company. Coenraad Jacob Temminck, as director of Holland's premier museum, became curator of many collectanea, including a sizeable portion from the very same M. Le Vaillant we met in chapter 7. Other naturalists will tend to want to flatter you in the hopes of securing patronage for their own collecting expeditions.

For reasons arcane and perverse, people in the East, but also Africa to a lesser extent, believe powdered pangolin scales (which make up about 20 per cent of the animals' total mass) will help them with all manner of ailments. Eating their own fingernails would do just as well and would be a whole lot cheaper. Rhino horn, pangolin scale, human finger- or toenails, hair, even chicken feathers – it's all the same stuff.

Of concern to the KEEP (Kalahari Endangered Ecosystem Project) people at Tswalu, where poaching is not an issue, is what pangolins along with the resident pygmy falcons, Cape cobras and boomslangs, barn owls, bat-eared foxes, various rodents and sociable weavers eat. In big-picture terms KEEP is concerned about climate change and the effects of changing climate and rainfall on what their animals do – or will – have to eat.

Take the pangolins, which are among the fussiest eaters among mammals. Should the Kalahari get even hotter and drier than it already is, the few ant and termite species on which they feed could disappear, and then so will they. The myremecophagists feed almost entirely at night so, although there might be other food species they could seek out in daytime, these walking artichokes cannot cope with extended exposure to harsh sunshine.

People lucky enough to get to see them might also be entertained by the unexpected behaviour of seeing them walking on their hind legs. What was that saying about seeing a dog walking on its back legs, that it is surprising it is done at all? The thing is, unlike dogs, pangolins do it very well. Their front legs are much like our arm and hands, having adapted in design primarily for digging in hard ground to break open ant and termite nests.

When walking on all fours, because of their long front claws, they walk on the outsides of their "hands". And while they are more than capable of digging their own nest burrows, they far prefer to use those abandoned by aardvarks.

Once broken into, their long and sticky tongues probe the labyrinthine earthworks, basically gluing on their food. That tongue is about as long again as the animal's own body and is attached to its thorax and not its trachea, as is normally the case with mammals. Having keratinous spikes on the inside of their stomachs compensates their lack of teeth. Like crocodiles and some birds, they ingest stones which help to grind up the food in their stomachs.

Fun fact about pangolin scales: In Asia they were used in historical times as armour plating. In 1876 the Maharaja of Datia presented an entire suit of armour made of gilded pangolin scales to the Prince of Wales – later King Edward II – during a tour of India. Each small scale was first copper plated and then edged with a floral design in gold. Larger scales were further given a jewelled border comprised shards of ruby, ivory, sapphire, pearls, ivory and coloured glass.

AARDVARKS ARE CLASSED AMONG THE living fossils, their lineage having split off and changed little for the past 160 million years. If you want to sound erudite on safari, the next time anyone trots out that old aphorism about hyraxes being the closest living relatives of elephants, you can add: "Yes, along with elephant shrews, manatees, dugongs, golden moles and aardvarks."

The old literature gives them the English name ant bear, but that is highly inappropriate because in no way do they resemble bears. Ant pig, or earth pig, would be better, if you had to have one. We are happy with aardvark, which has to be the very best word in the modern English lexicon.

As with all other myremecophagists, they can be found wherever there are termites, which is pretty much wherever you find grass and trees. They might look clumsy, but they can get up a fair head of steam when pursued. If overrun, they'll flip over onto their backs and then beware that front-end earthmoving equipment!

Adults weigh about as much a small adult human, albeit a chubby one since their bodies are no more than a metre long (the hefty tail adds a substantial loading on a scale). You'd think they couldn't do much anything at speed, but you'd be wrong about that. They are the bane of many people whose fields they dig up. The mammalian reference equivalent of *Roberts*, Smithers, notes a mealie farmer who was seen to grab one by the tail and get dragged for about 50 metres before letting go.

But they seem to prefer burrowing into the compacted ground of gravel roads and earthen dams. Farmers learn at their expense that an aardvark can out-dig even the most determined team with picks and shovels. Reay Smithers, author of the definitive text on Southern African mammals,[25] recorded a case in Zimbabwe where just such a gang chased an animal as it dug, but eventually gave up the contest after having trenched more than 30 metres.

The babies (cubs? piglets? Now there's a Trivial Pursuit corker)[26] are born with a full set of mammalian teeth in order to eat a varied

---

[25] Reay Smithers, *The Mammals of the Southern African Subregion*, University of Pretoria, 1983.
[26] They can be called calves or cubs.

diet. However, by adulthood they have only "cheek teeth" at the back of their jaw – but which lack enamel. They could chew, but why bother when you have a muscular gizzard-like stomach where your soft food is ground to a paste.

Highly developed salivary glands almost entirely encircle their necks and ensure their tongues, which give pangolins a go in the measuring game, are continually coated with thick, gummy saliva. Also, like pangolins, they are not so good at seeing or hearing, but their sense of smell is uncanny.

Where our noses have three blades of bone called the nasal conchae, whose function is to filter and regulate the temperature and humidity of the air we breathe, aardvarks have 10. They also have nine olfactory bulbs in their forebrains, which is the most of any mammal.

These earth pigs eat both termites and ants wherever they can, but avoid army, driver, red and Matabele ants, which give back as good as they are given. The termite mounds of their home territories alone cannot provide their prodigious calorific needs, so at night they go on the search for columns of termites or ants that are on the move.

Once again here we turn to Smithers for the facts: he records someone following an aardvark on the prowl for 6.5 kilometres while it hoovered up insects. The evidence from the stomach contents of 20 animals (what scientists have to do!) showed some contained more scarab beetles, others more ants, others more termites, so it seems they eat whichever is available. One offered up a fat mouse (*Steatomys pratensis*), but the mammologist author reckons "it must have been ingested fortuitously".

If ever you've taken public transport through the backveld, invariably you will have been offered deep-fried termite cakes, along with mice skewers and possibly pangolin on a stick by vendors who'll rap at your window wherever there is a bus or taxi stop. They are highly nutritious and, at least as far as mzungus are concerned, have a taste and texture far more appealing than that of mopane worms, wet or dried.

They are scooped up in great quantities whenever they emerge as flying alates.

Given their overwhelming abundance, what with the current rush to make laboratory foods, they could provide a viable alternative to feedlot-farmed meats, soy boerewors or frakenburgers.

Those cakes taste a lot like crunchy peanut-butter cookies.

An Inordinate Fondness for Tortoises

WE SOUTHERN AFRICANS SEEM TO have an inordinate fondness for tortoises. It might well be a result of this region being host to around 30 per cent of the total world species count, and most of those live only here. How often have you seen a padloper walking down, or across, a lonely country road and possibly stopped to give it a leg over to the side of the road? Many of us did, and some possibly still do, keep them as pets (although we shouldn't). They are just so non-judgemental. And so endearing.

Just to be clear, all tortoises are turtles, just like all toads are frogs. If you count you'll find there are 27 species of the order Chelonia found in Southern Africa. Of those, five are sea or marine turtles and another eight are either terrapins or mud turtles (freshwater turtles). Which leaves us with 13 or 14 species (depending on who is counting species or sub-species) of the things we down here in the real deep south call a tortoise, skilpad or ufudu. Those are the ones we're talking about. In some other places people call them land turtles.

I named my first Kombi camper "Ufudu" because it was a hard-shelled home on four pads, which might also be the reason I chose to showcase them in this book. It's a more likely and noble reason than another, of which I am deeply ashamed: chopping a pet tortoise in half to see what was inside. I blame my parents, who should have known better than to give an endangered creature to a curious five-year-old. Then again, some people do call them mobile meat pies and lots of animals, including people, love to crunch on them.

The Khoi and the San used them – the meat and the shells –

extensively. Some birds eat them: ground hornbills, for example, will swallow small ones whole. There are stories about lammergeiers (ossifrages) dropping them from a height, as they are known to do with bones, to break them open and nosh on the insides. There's a story about the lammergeier that dropped a tortoise onto the bald head of ancient Greek playwright Aeschylus and killed him. Imagine that: there you are sauntering along in the Drakensberg, humming a tune like the Singing Nun, when suddenly…!

Some years back I was camping at Rooiwal in the Baviaanskloof. I'd been for a walk followed by a swim in the refreshing Kouga River, and was propped up against a rock on a sandy beach reading-dozing. I'd been impressed by the sizeable population of large mountain tortoises so was not unduly surprised when one, about the size of a beach ball (do people still have beach balls?) came lumbering past me to the water's edge. Going for a drink, I thought, even though the literature says they don't much. Then it plunged right into the racing current.

I jumped up in alarm and watched it bob off downstream. Trying to race it running along the riverbank was in vain, it was moving too fast and the bush was too dense and thorny. I felt I had let it down and would one day have to answer for my dereliction of duty. Attempts to try to read were shot through with guilt and images of a dead tortoise floating around in the dam downstream.

So imagine my surprise when, sometime later, another tortoise of about equal size came waddling past me – they can move at a good pace when they want to – walked right into the river and raced off downstream. Was it the same one that had hit on a really cool adventure sport, or were they doing relay races here?

I spent some research time in the summer of '85, crawling around one of few remaining tracts of renosterveld up in the Swartland, near the Voëlvlei Dam, looking for tortoises. Once upon a time renosterveld covered much of the low-lying land of the southwestern Cape, from the northern slope of Devil's Peak into the Swartland – an area defined by the more fertile soils of the fynbos biome. Today 95 per cent of it is gone to urban expansion, wheat fields and vineyards. Black rhinos used to love it there, but were likely the first large animals to be rendered extinct in the region.

Nowadays just about every species endemic to this habitat is on its way out, including the diminutive geometric tortoise (*Psammobates geometricus*) for which I was searching. Along with the similar looking tent tortoise, it is surely the most attractive of its kind. The IUCN Red Data List has it pegged as Critically Endangered and facing extinction.

I did find a few but that was a long time ago now; its unlikely many people will ever again get to see them in the plural, if at all. Unfortunately, that is the likely fate of many of our ufudus, with the exception of some species that have wider distributions, including most of the padlopers and mountain species. The latter is also known as the leopard tortoise because, when young, they have distinctive black-and-yellow markings on their carapaces. That's the top, domed part of the shell, with the plastron underneath. The shell is composed of flattened ribs, which means it no longer has any need for an internal support structure.

All the species found in the sub-continent fall into the suborder Crytodira or hidden-necked tortoises, being able to fully retract their necks and heads into their shells (unlike those giant long-necked ones found on Pacific and Indian Ocean islands). South Africa has two "centres of endemism", or biological hot spots, of chelonids. One is the Mpumalanga and KwaZulu-Natal lowveld where terrapins abound. The other is the Eastern and Western Cape for land turtles. While they can live in harsh environments, none are found in Lesotho or the surrounding highlands.

The leopard or mountain species (*Stigmochelys pardalis*) is our largest and most widespread and the geometric is the rarest, while our smallest tortoise is the Cape speckled padloper, *Chersobius signatus* (formerly *Homopus* sp.). Males grow up to 8 centimetres and females 10 centimetres (the size and shape of a small bread roll) and, unlike most other species with noticeably domed carapaces, the padloper species (there are five of them) are easily recognised by their small size and flattened carapace. Luckily for them there are no ground hornbills around the southern or Little Namaqualand where they occur. But unlucky for them they are prized by collectors, and frightfully endangered in the wild. In fact, all our tortoises are protected by law and should not be collected, but you know people!

Our most famous tortoise was Domkrag (car jack), a resident of the Addo Elephant National Park for maybe as long as 100 years, which hit the scales at around 40 kilograms. Stories were that he would shuffle under cars and slowly raise the front or rear axle. One day the reptilian weightlifter fell down an aardvark hole and died when he couldn't get out. Last time I was there his shell was on display outside the rest camp interpretation centre.

TORTOISES ARE POLYGAMOUS AND DOMINANT males get to mate more often than less aggressive ones. Invariably the courtship period can be frenetic, at a kind of tortoise pace. If two males locate a female giving off the right scent, they will approach one another with heads bobbing, issuing hissing and growling sounds, raise themselves to full height and then lunge at one another. They'll use their heads and necks to try to flip the rival, but they also have a hidden weapon.

You might notice that males have a spur that projects from the front of their plastron; it's called a gular scute or scale. The bigger the gular the better chance a tortoise has of inflicting serious wounds in its opponent, tearing skin and even breaking bits of the shell. All spoils to the victor.

But females can also be aggressive and generally some argy-bargy ensues before mating commences. The male will circle his intended, nodding his head, ramming her, biting her legs (more like gumming really) and attempting to trap her against some obstacle. She will lunge back and try to make off, while he pushes her around. Eventually she'll give in, or up, or else there'd be no tortoises.

Like all other reptiles, as well as their relatives the birds, both male and female tortoises have only one in-out plumbing hole called a cloaca. A male has a tail longer than a female's, his plastron is concave and the rear end of his carapace curves inwards. The female's plastron is flat and her rear carapace curves outwards. This allows the male to mount the female and get his cloaca to align with hers. Mating is often a noisy business with the male grunting while he stamps his hind feet on the ground.

Aside from collecting and loss of habitat, one of the most serious threats to these slow-rolling creatures is veld fires. The bottommost "hot wire" of electrified farm fences also wreak a heavy toll. Roads with steep edges form insurmountable barriers to their movement, while those with high curbs can become death traps. And then there's the traffic itself: some people think it's a game to run over wild creatures in their way. People!

But even Good Samaritans can do more harm than good trying to move tortoises from possible danger. These animals store water in a sack, or bursa, inside their cloaca, which helps them to live in arid environments. One of their defences, especially when being picked up, is to expel fluid – which could also mean handing it a death sentence. Should that happen you need to help it regain the lost liquid, but many wild tortoises will not drink from a bowl (no one taught them how). What you need to do is place it in a bowl of lukewarm water up to the plastron, so it can absorb water up the cloaca and into its bursa.

Best is to just leave them, unless you find one on a busy road or one with a hazardous curb. But whatever you do, just don't try to see what's inside.

Big Bertie's Broken Heart

BACK IN THE LATE 1980s my mate Donald and I, with our respective wives, decided we wanted to go and live and work in the Okavango Delta. We found positions managing twin safari camps Xakanaxa and Tsaro respectively. We had many adventures, the animals were generally compliant and could be relied on to earn their keep, but some of the guests could be extremely hard work. Hardly a day went by we could say was boring, indeed far from it.

High up on the list of entertainment were the two American businessmen who arrived with two extremely sexy partners, who turned out to be Russian prostitutes. The tricky part was keeping the peace when the two women decided they were above that, and refused to provide the services for which they had been engaged.

Then there was the boor who thought he had a right, even a duty, to insult just about everyone at the dinner table. We eventually booked a flight without his knowledge, took him on a game drive past the airstrip, stopped there and escorted him onto the plane. "Tell your travel agent to send us the bill," we said as we bade him good riddance.

But one incident that looms among the largest is the long and kinky saga of big Bertie[27] and how to get him home. A popular chocolate-bar manufacturer had booked out the lodges over a long weekend, as an incentive trip to reward its salespeople, as companies will do rather than forfeit all that sweet lolly to the taxman.

One of the chosen was Bertie, a man who had clearly developed a deep and lasting relationship with the company's products. Getting him in and out of the game drive vehicles provided camp staff and fellow guests with ample opportunities for exercise. Poor Bertie's

---

[27] Not his real name.

petite wife exhibited equal amounts of concern and unease with each boarding and disembarkation.

She fussed over him like a mother hen, while his colleagues expressed concern for his welfare. It was clear everyone was on eggs waiting for an explosion of some kind from Bertie's end. He smoked and he drank and he ate far too much. The Saturday night was when they held their main celebration party and everyone went big, but none bigger than Bertie. The staff had to help him to his bungalow. Early on the Sunday morning Mrs Bertie informed the office, apologising that they would not be able to make the scheduled game drive. Bertie had passed.

In retrospect the easiest part was dealing with her, when she became all matter-of-fact and seemed more than happy to be put on an early flight from Khwai River Lodge (which had an all-weather airstrip, able to carry her away from all the fuss and bother, in a fancy King Air twin-engined turbo-prop) back to Johannesburg. It was just as well she was not around to witness the harrowing events that followed.

To be blunt, Bertie was enormous, and now he was a dead weight. The first hurdle was to get his vast and inert body into a Land Rover and drive it to nearby Khwai River Lodge on the other, east, side of North Bridge, all the while trying to play down the situation. It took four strong staff to accomplish phase one.

The next challenge was transferring Bertie into the single-engine, six-seater Beechcraft that was the air taxi at Khwai, and fly him to Maun for air and border clearance. Even for smaller, more mobile people, getting in and out of these light planes can be challenging. Getting the Michelin Man in was a most undignified and exhausting procedure: not the kind of thing you'd want to do more often than was absolutely necessary. Or want the wife to see.

A small army of people heaved and dragged and pushed and shoved and forced the departing guest into the middle row of seats, bent some body parts, then forced the doors closed on the bloated body. It brought to mind those special platform employees on the Tokyo underground who have to shove in all the bodies and body parts as the doors close: but done African bush style.

The resident pilot, Moose Miller[28] was the most experienced birdman around the Delta at the time. He'd made the trip from Khwai to Maun many times and assumed that stopping to clear customs there would be the mere formality en route to Johannesburg it had been on countless other flights. It turned out to be one of those days when a thing we assume trips us up.

Miller landed with his usual panache and taxied to the parking space closest to the terminal building, in the full glare of the sun in hot and dry October, the notorious suicide month in safariland. That turned out to be his second error of judgement on the day.

The pilot jumped out and took his and his passenger's passports, for what on any other day would have been a mere formality of border etiquette, pilot and customs officials being so well acquainted, and this being such a humdrum formality, on a hot and slow Sunday. The customs officer on duty on the day was having none of it and asked where the passenger Bertie X was. He was not satisfied that Bertie was in the plane; he had to present himself in real live person.

We have a problem, Houston. Maybe the customs man was grumpy for having to work the weekend shift, or had a really bad hangover, or maybe had got into a fight with his wife, or had had a run-in with his boss, or perhaps he was just one of those obtuse officials you come across from time to time. Whatever, he was not acting true to type or local custom.

It was explained, with Oscar-worthy mime enactments, that Bernie was not very well disposed to present himself at the desk: was ill, in fact he was extremely ill, if the truth be revealed and urgently needed to get home. Miller did all he could to explain that it was a delicate situation, but the more the pilot protested the more insistent the customs man became.

The pilot eventually had to come clean and admit his passenger was in fact dead and was not in any state to present himself at the desk. Which was just what the wily customs man had suspected. Even when Miller implied that it was going to go from bad to worse if he could not execute an "emergency" repatriation, the customs man would not be swayed. Not even when the pilot implied this might be a

---

[28] Also not his real name.

good time for the customs official to bend his ways, either financially or physically depending.

But the custodian of the forces of all that was right and regular stood firm and declared that, in that case, the subject could not leave the country until a death certificate had been signed. So off Moose went, to find the only doctor in town and get the death certificate, leaving Bertie in the plane on the runway, in the unimpeded power of the African sun, a situation that was soon to become the hottest subject of this frontier town.

Remember, this was Maun back in the late 1980s. After a not very lengthy search the doctor was tracked down inside the shade and coolth of the town's favourite tavern. After some time diving and ducking, the man insisted that he could not sign a death certificate without first conducting a post mortem but, this being the Sabbath, he would be able to do so only the following morning, a regular working day.

The patrons of "The Duck", being possibly the most democratic institution in all of Ngamiland, held an impromptu referendum, after which it was agreed: the following morning would be the best, indeed the only reasonable, time to conduct the required medical procedure. Things should be done by the book, it was agreed. In gratitude for the support of his peers, the good doctor volunteered (possibly unknowingly) to buy a round.

Maun, also one of the most notoriously rowdy towns of the region at the time, was a place few people washed up in by choice. Most were running away from something and if it was not the law or money lenders, it was a cuckolded lover or sometimes demons of a more psychological nature. A movie should be made about the place.

When the sun lowered its brow and the temperature dropped from roasting to merely baking, it was decided that the "patient" should be moved to the mortuary, outside of which there were at least a few mopane trees offering paltry shade to the prefab building. In the meantime, Donald had driven the arduous track from North Bridge to Maun, and he manoeuvred his tired old Land Rover alongside the plane in which Bertie reclined.

With help from the airport porters the indisposed man was pulled and pushed and bent out of the aeroplane and placed on the load-bed of the Land Rover with the tail gate down and legs sticking out the back. This being Maun, on a Sunday, it was deemed that a red rag tied around one of the big toes might be deemed to be offensive. You just never knew with authority.

Of course, Bertie could not be left overnight in the back of the Land Rover, what with all manner of night lurkers in a place on the edge of the wilderness. So he was carried inside and placed on a stainless steel table in the middle of the rudimentary mortuary building with no ceiling or air conditioning and left there to stew.

The following morning pilot, safari manager and mortuary assistant were at the appropriate place at opening time. The doctor arrived a mere hour later. Lucky for Bertie he was already dead, so the fact that the doctor was not full steady on his legs was of only passing concern. The safari guest need not have feared any damage to his now well-stiffened body. After fiddling around for some time, the doctor finally admitted he was not qualified to carry out post-mortems and promptly set off for the inn.

What to do? Once again big Bertie was loaded onto the back of the small Land Rover, legs protruding, then taken back to the airport and stuffed back inside the cramped Beechcraft. This time some more forceful manipulation of the limbs was required – in full view of the control tower and all other interested bystanders.

Cargo duly loaded, Miller brushed down his uniform and headed for the customs office, two passports in hand, and presented them to the same customs man who had been on duty the previous day. The man had been observing the proceedings with keen interest.

"So where is this person?" he asked, pointing at Bertie's picture on the page of the open passport.

"In the plane," replied the pilot.

"I see him," said the customs man.

Thump! Thump! He stamped both passports and within minutes Miller and Bertie were airborne and heading for Lanseria Airport. Afterwards, sitting at the bar counter of Khwai River Safari Lodge, Miller could not recall whether or not the customs man had wished him a pleasant flight.

The Honeyguide Effect: A Mnemonic for Our Home in the Wilderness

"WE DON'T LOVE AFRICA BECAUSE it's safe," remarked our guide Grant, somewhat rhetorically. We were sitting under a giant sycamore fig on a bank of the Selinda Spillway in north-eastern Botswana, sipping cold St Louis beers and tucking into a lunch of freshly made pot bread, sosaties and salads, our heart rates having returned to normal. Up in the tree a greater honeyguide (*Indicator indicator*) issued its tell-tale, insistent *whit-prrr, whit-prrr*.

Our bedraggled group had gathered on the bank after meeting our Waterloo, or kubu, the local name for hippo. One of the canoes in our small flotilla had been upended by just one such kubu as we drifted lazily across its pool. We couldn't blame the hippo because, we figured, it would not previously have seen the sight of four large, cigar-shaped objects cutting across its aquatic ceiling. No one had died (bonus), so there we sat, bush hats drooped and dripping like wet slices of bread. Definitely not for sissies, we concurred.

The back-up crew had got there ahead of us but, being descendants of the Makalolo people, who'd paddled David Livingstone down the Zambezi to his fated appointment with Mosi-oa-Tunya (as they called the falls, which he subsequently went and named after some imperious ruler), knew to keep close to the bank and not paddle across the middle of a large pool, likely territory of a fickle kubu. (I suspect quite a few of the old explorers were covertly in search of peerages and none more so than Dr Livingstone.)

"Can water flow uphill?' asked someone in the group (I swear she was blonde, kind of strawberry blonde, no stranger to these parts and no fool either). Someone else chuckled, but it was not nearly so dumb a question as it might at first have seemed.

The Selinda Channel, down which we were paddling, flows out from the eastern edge of the immeasurable Okavago Delta at a place called Motswiri. It empties into Lake Zibadianja, into which also disgorges floodwaters of the smaller Linyanti wetlands from the north. From that ephemeral lagoon the Savuti Channel flows ever eastwards to the Savuti Marsh and, in times of exceptionally high water, into the Chobe River, which in turn flows into the mighty Zambezi.

If that's not already complicated enough, it gets more so. Sometimes the entire system, or parts of it, stop flowing, and even reverse direction, for no reason that is obvious to man or beast that have been witnessing it for centuries. The Selinda Spillway, for example, had not flowed for some decades but was now brim-full.

IT WAS AROUND MID-YEAR IN 2009 and I was between work (my family reckons I'm always between work) and wondering what to do next with my beggarly life, when my phone rang.

"Howzit, it's Colin."

"Hey Bell Boy, what's gives?"

"How would you fancy joining a small group to paddle down the Selinda Spillway?"

My mind's eye teleported me to a serpentine, dry waterway, seldom more than about 30 metres wide, with leadwood-lined, 3-metre-high banks. It snakes through a sea of mopane woodland somewhere near where the Caprivi sticks its thumb into Botswana's eye. When I'd last been there a decade previously it had been a 70-kilometre-long 4x4 game-viewing track. Back then the grass was high, trees were growing in the channel and it was hard to imagine flowing water had ever passed this way.

Failed missionary but superlative explorer, David Livingstone must have been driven by fires of passion not experienced by we ordinary people. Why else would he have abandoned his wife and children to the ravages of wild beasts, tsetse flies and mosquitoes on the shore of Lake Ngami and set off in search of the source of the

Nile? It's hard to track Livingstone's exact route from the time he left his family to their fate until he reached Victoria Falls in early 1852. However, from his own records we can tell he must have skirted the Okavango Delta.

In his diary, published in 1857, he notes: "The Teoughe and Tamunal'le,[29] being essentially the same river, can never outrun each other. If either could we then have the phenomenon of a river flowing two ways; but this has never been observed to take place here, and it is doubtful it can ever occur in this locality."

He never mentions the Selinda Spillway, but then why should he, since that is not its African name? Also, records of the time suggest it was not flowing but would have been a grassy passage, much as I remembered it. Some decades later, however, hunter Frederick Courteney Selous noted it was flowing strongly and posed a significant barrier to his progress. So, what cuts with these rivers that seem to flow every which way, whenever nature pleases?

One clue to the capricious nature of the Selinda Spillway is its local name, Magweqana, meaning "many small pools of water". This suggests that in recent decades, as in centuries past, the spillway has flowed, then stopped, receded to form hippo pools and then become a grassy memory, time and again.

We now know the entire region was once part of a vast and shallow inland sea that was fed by all the major rivers of south-central Africa. In fact, in times long past, the Zambezi was not the main river of the region. Tens of thousands of years ago the Zambezi was much smaller and flowed into the Okavango River system, and it fed a lake even larger than the one we see today as the endless flats of the Makgadikgadi Salt Pans. The story of how all that changed is pretty much the same as the one that plays out there today.

Over time, Livingstone and many others got their riempies in a tangle trying to figure out how the enigmatic wetlands, rivers and channels seemed to defy logic and the very laws of nature as they are understood. They'll flow this way for a few years, or decades, cease flowing and dry up, and then start flowing the other way. Yet even the

---

[29] Almost certainly the Thamalakane River, the main channel that drains the Delta and runs southwards through Maun.

ancients knew water does not flow uphill without divine intervention.

A 1998 Botswanan government water report states: "The hydrology of the Savuti Marsh is dominated by only one process – the occasional spill from the Linyanti Swamp during times of high water in the Linyanti-Chobe river systems. That source has not flowed for more than a decade now. The Savuti Channel has in fact ceased to exist."

Clearly those government hydrologists had not done a very thorough search of the literature. Research over the past four decades reveals that from around 120#000 to about 17#000 years BP[30], what has been called Lake Paleo-Makgadikgadi, once covered almost all of northern Botswana. The origins of this great lake are believed to be a combination of much higher rainfall and tectonism.

AND THERE IT WAS IN clear science speak: increased flow (floods) and earthquakes. Recent geological research reveals that the entire Ngamiland region is underscored by a network of hairline cracks in the bedrock, upon which rests a deep cushion of Kalahari sand. These fractures in the Earth's crust are the most south-westerly extension of the Great Rift Valley. When Africa burps the bedrock rumbles, almost imperceptibly, and the ground shakes and shivers. Those deep Kalahari sands shift almost imperceptibly, as if some Titan was shaking a giant sugar bowl.

The rise and fall across the entire country is only several hundred metres. So, when the sugar bowl shakes, it sends water lying on the surface flowing every which way. A river that previously flowed from the Okavango down the Selinda Spillway, or down the Savuti Channel into the Savuti Marsh and thence on towards to the Chobe River, might cease flowing, pause a while to consider the lie of the land, and then change its mind along with its direction. There is no hard data but it does seem to happen about once every several decades, give or take.

"Hey, Davey boy, are you still there?"

"Oh, ja, sorry Col, I was just thinking."

My caller was an old acquaintance and safari fundi.

---

[30] Before present, same as BCE – before current epoche – essentially BC.

"Well, do you fancy joining us? We'll be the first people to paddle the Selinda Spillway in 35 years."

He estimated the two waterways would meet sometime in early July, in less than two weeks' time. If I wanted to see this natural phenomenon I'd better start blowing up my waterwings.

Some 10 days later I was entertaining an aching back from three days of sustained paddling, but elated to be drifting down this legendary channel when I might otherwise have been, I dunno, working perhaps. Hippos snorted explosively as we slid by, jacanas hopped around on the waterlily pads, larger birds plied the living trade route with the heady aroma of wild sage permeating the air.

In the early evening a breeding herd of about 20 elephants emerged from the green-gold curtain of riverine bush on the bank ahead, where the channel made a 90-degree turn.

"There's a big bull elephant on our right that wants to cross the channel just ahead of us; we need to give him space," our guide cautioned.

The big boy caught our scent and hesitated. Then he plunged in shoulder-deep, ploughing diagonally across our line. He moved unexpectedly swiftly, directly towards the herd. As he approached, a younger male broke away from the group to confront him. We all held our formation, and our collective breath ... but instead of a crunching of ivory and elephant bone, the two bulls entwined raised trunks and trumpeted with obvious joy. This was not the territorial joust we were anticipating, but the reunion of old friends, probably family, separated by the vagaries of seasons and cycles of flood and famine.

A RAINDROP FALLS SOMEWHERE IN Angola, finds itself on the salient of some highland and begins a new journey as moving water. Along the way it is joined by innumerable others, all captured in that same catchment and rushing southwards towards the Okavango River, slowing down as they wend a course through the serpentine Panhandle, crossing the Gumare fault line and then coming to a virtual standstill and splaying out into the world's largest inland delta.

Months later, acted upon by forces both cosmic and atomic, they follow the line of least resistance and exit at a place marked on maps as Motswiri, gushing through the gape of the Selinda Spillway, for which the sensation of flowing water is a welcome delight. Following decades of famine, the feast returns.

Some way to the east, halfway across the sub-continent, another rain droplet falls and it finds its way into the Kwando River. It crosses the Caprivi Strip and eventually reaches the Linyanti wetland. There, instead of taking the well followed path to the Chobe River, it veers south and west, into Lake Zibadianja. From there, there would be two options, depending on the most minute balance of probabilities. Ours follows an antediluvian pathway to the eastern opening into the Selinda Spillway, which also has not felt the soothing caress of running water for some span, time that is cyclic yet unpredictable.

Those two little drops race to a covalent conclusion and meet with innumerable others as they swirl along Selinda in the time-old dance of resurrection. The spillway's ancient voice calls us and we paddle through its temporal portal, moving both backwards and forwards at once.

One morning we are again measuring our lives in paddle strokes and dove calls: "Work slowly", "drink lager", when someone in the lead canoe turns and calls.

"WTF was that!?"

By the time the rest of us have surfaced into the current moment we have all passed the "thing".

It takes some strenuous back-paddling into the current to locate the thing and paddle around it. We had drifted over a complete elephant skeleton with its tusks still intact. In the tea-coloured water it looked like – and felt to us like – some fantastical creature frozen in artesian amber.

Another tree, another lunch stop, another story. Kasane-based Grant recalled his own campfire conversations with a Bayei tracker from these parts. The man told him how, when he was a child, each winter when the water was high, he would accompany his father and grandfather in the family mokoro on hunting trips. From their home at Seronga they would head down the Savuti Channel, across Lake Zibadianja and up into the Linyanti wetland to hunt hippos. They would dry the meat, load the dugout to the gunwales and pole all the way back again before the annual floodwaters receded.

The last hunt would have taken place in the early 1970s, which was when the annual floods began to ebb, and the retreating water in the channel began making the journey ever more arduous. By about 1980 both it and the Selinda Spillway had shrunk to many small pools of water.

"I first saw the Selinda Spillway about a decade later," Grant recounted. "By then only a few pools remained, forcing a mass of hippos into tight rafts that reached from bank to bank. By early 2003 the spillway was bone dry and Zibadianja Lagoon (as well as the Savuti Marsh) was a wide grazing paddock for game. The last stinking ooze of water could be seen from the air as a star-shaped depression, with the surviving hippos squeezed in nose to tail." A humanitarian appeal on behalf of the hippos was answered and the Department of Water Affairs opened a passage to the Kwando River.

The next year drought conditions worsened, the worst on record, and it was feared there might be no annual flood at all to deliver any small reprieve. However, in the first week of 2005 Grant noticed that the Spillway had started to flow, with no appreciable rainfall to account for it. But he had a theory.

He marked Christmas and New Year of 2004 as genesis of the current situation. Selinda Camp, where he was working at that time, had no bookings so he'd invited some friends to join him. They were leaning on the leadwood balustrade, sipping ales (rains that had held off rendered searing temperatures of mid-summer) when they heard – and felt – a low rumbling. A herd of stampeding buffs, they all thought at the same time. "We looked out across the dry bushveld but we couldn't see any buffaloes, nor the tell-tale dust plume they would have thrown up."

Far away, people sunning themselves on islands around the Indian Ocean at the time remember it all too well as the great tsunami that changed so many lives and attitudes about the forces of nature. Grant remembers the effect lasting about 30 seconds. A few weeks later the safari guide noticed a tentative trickle of water reaching out from Zibidianja Lagoon into the mouth of the Spillway.

When shock waves from the epicentre of the earthquake made landfall on the East African coastline a geological spasm nudged the sleeping giant that is the Great Rift Valley. It shrugged, threw up some dust and, as it settled, bumped the substrate just enough to send a riffle into the cracks lying as much as 1 000 metres under the Kalahari.

Like a sudden heart tremor in the bedrock, it opened a constricted artery, sending life-giving liquid down senescent veins that had been dry for so long, resuscitating a wrinkled body of red Kalahari dune sand that had been all but left for dead.

Still backwaters in the Okavango and Linyanti rippled, then began to tremble, then to flow, almost imperceptibly at first, awakening ancient pathways. Three-and-a-half years later the many pools had begun to coalesce and the last tracts of dry ground in between were quivering with anticipation. With it came elephants and hippos, antelope by the score, flocks of birds in their thousands, insects by the millions, and a honey-loving bird, all celebrating the great dance of the desert.

Our lunch demolished, we leaned back in our camp chairs (placed calf-deep in the stream) as the honeyguide launched from its perch and hovered overhead, darting back and forth in the air, insisting we follow it to wild honey somewhere in the woodlands beyond. After several minutes of urgent calling, it flew off in search of a more deserving audience, a honey badger perhaps, or a hunter-gatherer.

It is a well documented symbiotic relationship and legend has it that, if you follow the bird to a wild bee nest and don't leave it some honey, or wax filled with bee larvae, it will lead you to the hole of a mamba or den of a lion. The Bayei camp staff, whose forebears have hunted and gathered here since before the Great Flood, insisted it was no mere fable.

Mzungus have not cared much to understand the deeper rhythms of Africa. Only a pitiful few can speak an African language (not counting Afrikaans). From the time when the first caravels from Lisbon dropped anchor off a southern Cape shore, they've been extremely busy filling up with water and fresh meat, carving out colonies, erecting fences and paving highways. But we've done precious little to open ourselves to the rich spirit world that defines the lives of the people who have dwelt here since Mohlodi, the creator, left his footprints in the mountains.

Their, our (for naturally I count myself among the pale interlopers) family names do not celebrate the wild creatures: we don't have our animal totems like zebra (dube), elephant (ndlovu) or crocodile (ngwenya). We do not consult with the ancient spirits – the shades – in times of need or doubt, to placate demons or celebrate our joys. We don't venture into the mountains to pluck the delicate everlastings, imphepha, and burn or boil them in order to release their powers in smoke or steam. We do not dance the land or sing its praises much.

There have always been exceptions, people like David Livingstone who was a dismal failure as a missionary but fell under Africa's spell. In turn he was virtually worshipped by the indigenous people with whom he consorted, not as a holy person but as a man with exceptional empathy. Or Adrian Boshier, the English-born eccentric who relocated with his family to South Africa and fell under its spell. Boshier failed to qualify as a sangoma but was recognised by his African mentors as a man of exceptional spiritual power. They, the sangomas of the bushveld, named him Rradinoga, father of snakes.

But sometimes, when even we ordinary folk travel with open minds, we catch a glimpse of the spirits around us, sometimes right beneath our feet, when we are so busy adding numbers and counting beans, standing at counters or having our cars filled with fuel.

Sitting round the campfire the night of our hippo and honeyguide encounter, well fed and watered, I reflected on our current journey and tried to make sense of the deep feelings it had stirred in all of us. I recalled an incident some years earlier when I was a guest at one or other lodges in the Linyanti area (it was likely King's Pool, operated by a certain specific safari company, given what followed).

The guests were gathered around the fire after dinner. A woman in fashionable safari attire asked the host if the camp had wi-fi (a new-fangled thing at the time, not much seen in the bush).

No.

What about email?

No again.

Cell phone reception?

Negative.

How could the company be so negligent, she demanded to know. What if there was an emergency at her home? The guide was schtum, but I just could not refrain.

Because this is the wilderness: the clue is right there in the camp's name. The whole idea being that we turn off our city personas and tune into the sounds and spirit of the bush. Needless to say, she dismissed me as she would an annoying bug.

But camped there beside our inscrutable waterway, I felt the well ordered lives that awaited us back in our towns and cities were no more worthy than what we had there: a fire, food, a tent, bucket shower and Doug, the mobile toilet. Grant was right in observing that we love Africa for the adventure it offers, but I think it goes much deeper than that. The scent of wild sage and wood smoke gave me a sense of being in a place of safety, rather than fear.

Still today, a canoe safari down a mysterious waterway named Selinda plays like a mnemonic to remind me that it was not a mere holiday, or escape from my urban groove, but a return to a primordial home. I think of it as the honeyguide effect: follow me, it insists, and I will lead you to the sweetness. Trust me and I'll take you back to your proper place in the wilderness.

The shades know this to be true. *Whitt-prrrrr, whitt-prrrrr.*

Ladies and Gentlemen, We Present, the Beetles and the Rolling Dungballs!

PEOPLE WHO STUDY INSECTS PROBABLY turn up their noses each time that old observation of JBS Haldane's is rolled out, about God's fondness for stars and beetles, like there's poo on their shoe. The thing about clichés, though, is that invariably they are based on some truism. Of stars we know there are untold billions: beetle numbers, being nowhere near that order of magnitude, are still impressive.

The order of Coleoptera, beetles, is a subdivision of the super-order Endopterygota, which includes all things that go through larval, pupal and adult stages of metamorphosis.[31] The coleops are distinguished from the likes of moths, butterflies, flies, fleas, ants, bees and wasps, by benefit of having their front wings (elytra) hardened into wing cases.

When it comes to the numbers, there are about 400 000 species of beetles known, with more popping out just about every time anyone looks closely under some piece of tree bark or leaf litter. Coleoptera account for about 40 per cent of all known insect species, and a whopping one quarter of all the known kinds of animal life. Mammal species, by contrast, make up no more than 4 per cent.

As you might imagine the order of beetles is divided into various suborders, super-families, families and subfamilies. The biggest

---

[31] Some species go through multiple developmental stages of metamorphosis during their larval phase, the stages being called instars. Their specific number and speed of development is less species dependent than environmental, such as diet and temperature.

suborder is Polyphaga with 170 families, some of the main ones being the rove beetles, blister beetles, stag (including rhino) beetles, weevils and scarab beetles (Scarabaeidae, also called a super-family) of which there are more than 300 000 species.

Following the branching of their family tree there are many types of scarabs, including rain beetles, enigmatic scarabs, sand-loving scarabs, earth-boring ones, and then the true dung beetles, the subfamily Scarabaeinae with about 6 000 species worldwide. While it's true most of them eat mainly faeces, and are highly adapted to the task, some also feed on decaying vegetable matter and fungi (mushrooms). Within this there are those that specialise in – literally in – herbivore poop, while others prefer that of omnivores (such as pigs, primates – including us by the way – bears and dogs).

Of true dung beetles there are three main kinds, defined by what they do: rollers, dwellers and tunnellers, the last mentioned being by far the most numerous. There are an estimated 2 000 species in Africa, with about 800 in South Africa ranging from just a few millimetres to about 5 centimetres in length. Because of the habit of living either within a pile of dung, of burying the dung in tunnels in the ground beneath, these two groups are seldom seen and attract the least interest from both lay people and beetle researchers.

Beetle fundis reckon it was the fierce competition within the dung heap that drove some beetles to pack up their little parcels of excrement and roll them off to other less contested places. One group of the true dung beetles that is found mostly in Africa are those classified as *Sisyphus*, which have extraordinary long rear legs. They are named after the ancient Greek King of Ephyra who, having tried twice to trick the gods out of his own death, was forced to roll a large boulder to the top of a hill, only to have it roll back down before reaching the top … and so it goes on for eternity.

By far the most famous of all is the sacred scarab, *Scarabaeus sacer*, deified by the ancient Egyptians. They realised the dung rollers they saw used the sun to navigate to their home (turns out it's even more complex than that). When Khefri came to the throne of the Lower Kingdom, declaring the Sun God Ra to be the highest among all the deities, the humble dung beetle was elevated to his emissary on Earth.

Ladies and Gentlemen, We Present, the Beetles and the Rolling Dungballs!

If ever you have visited Egypt you'll know that, at all historical sites, there are people (mostly children) who will offer you a little gift, a token of their appreciation that you are visiting their country. Invariably it will be a little stone dung beetle. It is the law of the desert that one gift begets another; you can try to refuse but it will be in vain – these kids are pros. Of course, they want your money, but one strategy is to arrive with some other form of exchange, like ballpoint pens. A pocketful of scarabs is not the worst thing to take back home.

In Khefri's time it was not only the fact that the beetles rolled their balls parallel to the arc of the Sun across the firmament, but also that they buried their balls and then disappeared underground with them, new ones appearing in due time. For this culture, obsessed with death and re-incarnation, and who built huge temples to ensure safe passage in the afterlife, it was a big deal. The image of the scarab as a symbol of the rising sun, being swallowed by Nut at night, followed by renewal and resurrection each morning, become an all-pervasive symbol in the religious art of ancient Egypt.

There certainly is something beguiling about seeing a large beetle rolling its organic Pilates ball around the veld, and it's little wonder they also fascinate us veld lovers. It was only early in the 17th century that Italian naturalist Ulisse Androvandi uncovered the true nature of the ball: that it was in fact a brood ball in which the female laid her eggs, where the new beetles metamorphosed, ate the globular windfall and finally emerged into the open air as well-fed adults.

The falls of the Greek and Roman empires, and with them the collapse of effective sanitary systems throughout their respective regions of influence, highlighted the vital role of dung beetles in keeping the accumulated piles of human excrement at a tolerable level. An early English name for them was "tordwiffel", or turd weevil. And wouldn't you guess that humans, somewhere, would find a personal use – besides spiritual, ecological or scientific – for beetles that shovel shit, and that it would be the Chinese people. According to the official party-endorsed book on traditional medicines, the *Bencao Gangmu* or *Compendium of Mataeria Medica*, if eaten, dried dung beetle (qianglang) can cure at least 10 different ailments.

DUNG BEETLES HAVE TINY BRAINS, the vast majority of which are devoted to their miasmic skills: zoning in on fresh dung. They seem to much prefer freshly laid pats, although it is more likely that the strong odours emanating from a just-laid patty is much more attractive and easily found than an old dry one. Furthermore, fresh faeces are easier to work than dry and fibrous matter.

In one instance it was recorded that, within 15 minutes of an elephant defecating, 4 000 beetles had arrived on the scene. Within the hour they had been joined by another 12 000. If ever you have arrived at a fresh midden in the bush, the arrival of squadrons of flying olfactory machines can be unnerving. Much of that dung will find its way underground: adult and larval beetles will eat some, but a lot will remain to greatly enrich the soil all the while removing fetid clumps from soiling the surface.

Some beetle researchers reckon their subjects, along with ants and earthworms, constitute the three greatest living, mainly unobserved, transformers of the surface of the Earth (other than in the Antarctic where they do not occur but ice is active). It turns out that for humans these little night-soil movers are also among the most important non-vertebrates. Just ask an Australian what outdoor life was like there back in the day.

By the 1960s Australia's fly explosion had become unbearable to both humans and stock, what with their 300-plus species of dung beetles not doing a very good job of dealing with all the accumulated dung from all the introduced farmed animals. They, the indigenous beetles, had evolved to deal with the much drier, more fibrous faeces of marsupials. That of the newly arrived mammals – mainly sheep, cows and pigs – was much wetter, sloppier and far more copious.

As a result, there was an explosion of local bush flies, as well as imported (water) buffalo flies. Vast swathes of pastureland lay under a layer of festering animal waste. Studies by American pastureland scientists reveal that dung beetles save their own country around US$380 million a year by burying faeces on farms that would otherwise foul the fields and cause fly infestations.

In 1965 Hungarian-born zoologist George Bornamissza was put in charge of Australia's Dung Beetle Project, and he experimented with various beetle species from Africa and Europe. In the end two southern African species proved to be their best candidates for agricultural sewage control, so a dual programme was set up in South Africa.

Over time millions of beetles of 23 species (the eggs only, mind you, in order to avert importing other things including their gogga parasites) were exported to deal with Australia's poop windfall. By the time the cooperative endeavour was shut down, the Australians were recording vastly improved pasture health, along with a 90 per cent reduction in bush fly populations. No more cork hats, cobber.

Winston Churchill observed that all men were worms, but that at least he was a glow-worm. Likewise, while it is true all beetles are Coleoptera, some beetles could be called "glow beetles". The pin-up species for this accolade must go to *Scarabaeus satyrus*, which needs neither Sun nor Moon to guide it at night. How it got to be the centrespread on the walls of some entomology laboratories has a lot to do with the things scientists do.

Some of them can be extremely strange people, in a fishy kind of way. I remember in my student days doing experiments with intertidal creatures like tylos (sea lice), taking them from one side of the Cape Peninsula and putting them in pools on the other to see what they would do. What they did mainly was everything out of sync with their new tidal regime. And what a giant leap that was for the biological sciences!

Then there are those who have worked out how to make fish glow in the dark: not deep-sea varieties which do so naturally, but tank varieties such as goldfish and zebrafish. There was no reason to do this other than to see if they could. The lab geeks found a way to snip luminescent DNA from coral polyps and snap them into fish eggs. Maybe an actual use for them will be found one day, other than showing off your Frankenfish to your friends. Which is far better than blowing up frogs, making monkeys addicted to smoking, or chopping your pet turtle in half to see what it looks like inside, granted. Dung beetle biologists do much the same kind of thing, but arguably are not as cruel as what has been done to, say, rhesus monkeys in the name of science.

Nevertheless, some beetle studies still sound suspiciously like student pranks. One neat laboratory example is injecting dyes into beetle's cells to observe how individual light receptors are connected to the insect's nervous system. Presumably there'll be a use for that down the road for some aspect of robotics. (I believe it's being used in the development of a new generation of missiles, fancy that.)

Another is covering their feet with silicon shoes to see how they deal with hot surfaces, such as are encountered in desert regions where they occur. Some beetles live in places where daytime ground temperatures register up to 60°C, when most animals would go into heat distress as the ground hits 40°C. What they do is much the same as what lizards do: they dance in order to raise opposite sets of legs off the ground. The invertebrate rollers have the added benefit of being able to climb on top of their balls which, containing moisture, will be cooler than the surrounds.

Experiments revealed that both diurnal and nocturnal rollers climb up on their balls periodically to take a dead reckoning on the sky, in order to keep going in their intended direction. Even when the Sun was obscured the beetles seemed able to keep their internal GPSs on track. It was established, by fitting neat little paper peaked caps onto the beetles, that they could also navigate by using the angle of light polarisation (as can bees and some other insects). The hardest part was getting the caps to stay on since nothing seemed to stick to the beetles' carapaces. Solution: little paper chin straps.

One experiment called for painting the beetles' eyes with liquid Tippex, and why not? Apparently, the beetles did not seem to mind, or pay mind to, this intrusion and kept on rolling their balls like trolley pushers through rush hour traffic on garbage day. Their eyes are hard keratin, like human nails, so it did them little harm when the noble scientists scraped off the dried Tippex. I wonder if anyone thought to ask them how they *felt* about it?

How, though, some of the more determined among beetle savants wondered, did some manage to navigate at night when even the moon was not visible? Clearly more experiments were called for. Enter centre stage, *Scarabaeus satyrus*. But how do you design an experiment to figure out this one? Wits Professor Marcus Byrne[32] and some of his colleagues managed to convince the Johannesburg Planetarium to allow them to bring in their test subjects and play around with various night-sky perturbations. (I understand for this experiment the researchers were able to replace the dung with small plastic balls, which did not seem to deter the little rollers one faecal bit.)

What was found was that once a dung beetle has its ball it will set out in a straight line and not deviate for just about any obstacle short of a vertical wall (I have not as yet been able to learn why this is, and if they all set the same course). But to do it on a moonless night, with a brain smaller than a pin head? Turns out they use the stars: not any arbitrary star but the observable Milky Way, the central plane of our galaxy. It arches more or less vertically overhead during southern summers, the time when beetles are most reproductively active.

In 2013 this smart piece of scientific jiggery-pokery earned for Byrne and four collaborators an Ig Noble Prize in the combined category of botany-astronomy. The 23rd Ig Noble Prize ceremony, organised by the *Annals of Improbable Research*, was held at Harvard University and presented by actual Nobel laureates. The awards honour "achievements that first make people laugh, then make them think" (ig-noble, geddit?).

---

[32] Marcus Byrne and Helen Lunn, *Dance of the Dung Beetles*, Wits University Press, 2019.

Camp Life and Pets: They're Family But It Seldom Ends Well

Just about everyone who has lived in the bush will have had occasion to adopt some hapless creature that has, most often literally, fallen into their lap. Many are birds that have tumbled out of nests, but also bushbabies and African tree squirrels. The nest raiders might be mammal or bird, occasionally reptile, including boomslangs, baboons, monkeys and on occasion large-spotted genets (the small-spotted species being almost entirely ground-based), and birds ranging from hornbills to harrier hawks.

There can be few things more endearing than a tiny baby squirrel or galago, otherwise known as a bushbaby, when you hold its tiny beating body in your hands. The problems with raising them, however, are multiple, the most vexing – if you are a first-time adoptive parent – is what to feed them. In this regard mammals are much easier than birds since they will all drink milk in some form. It's therefore hard to kill them outright with kindness.

But baby birds are something of a different feather. Many people will assume that the young eat pretty much what the parents do but often they'd be wrong, especially in the case of seed-eaters. Baby birds need soft moist food, so trying to coax them with bird seed is only going to clog their innards. Moistened, good quality pet food is your general go-to for baby birds. Just try to make sure it's not one of those generic ones that contain "meat by-products" (unfit for human consumption), grains (which are used to bulk up the product), preservatives, dyes or any other synthetic ingredients.

In the case of most insect eaters, from flycatchers to swifts, the soft parts of insects should also work. Mealworms and broken-up hardboiled eggs are also good for general all round nosh; and don't forget a few drops of water every now and again administered with a dropper. Just remember to check, very gently, for breakages and general body functioning, since they might have had a hard bump on landing.

The best thing with a baby anything though is to try to put them back in their nest: forget that nonsense about parents rejecting offspring with human scent. On the other hand, it's no use putting a baby back in a nest if its parents have been eaten. If you cannot locate the nest, put them on a branch close to where they fell. Watch over it, and if no parent appears before dusk, he or she is all yours. Best of luck: baby birds need to be fed every 15 to 20 minutes.

I know a little about this from living under a dense umbrella of riverine trees for the best part of a year and finding all manner of creatures under it (from baby birds to full-grown black mambas). Many did not make it, but one that did, and stole everyone's hearts, was a teeny-weeny baby African tree squirrel. We found it on a path one morning after a bunch of rowdy baboons had swept through the canopy.

In the first few days of a very young squirrel's life hydration is even more important than food: a very weak solution of salt-and-sugar water should be dripped into its mouth. Once you start feeding the baby, you might need to stimulate its genital area and bum with something like an earbud, or else it might not be able to release waste (its mother would do this naturally). And, of course, keep the little thing warm.

The final word on feeding is to stay away from human milk products; rather try to use any animal milk product, fresh or powdered. This is all assuming there is no veterinary help close by.

One problem with these creatures is that they are of the wild, and should be sent back there as soon as they are able to fend for themselves. But sometimes we get too attached and the ending comes mostly tragically. Many are killed by other animals as they go about camp or begin to test the limits of their own bravery. Other times, with predators, they grow to become dangerous and have to be relocated or otherwise dispatched. Like my old uncle Ossie's favourite pet lion, Dandylion, who we met in chapter 1.

When baby Belhauser fell into our world, any professional help was a virtual expedition by land, or a two-hour flight away. She was named by one of our camp companions, Doug, most casually over a mealtime – not ours, the squirrel's. The staff invariably drifted into the dining lapa whenever we fed her – with tools, gardening or kitchen implements, or cleaning gear in their hands, to see how things were going and offer advice.

I married soon after graduating and, together with my new wife, set off to run a safari camp in the Okavango Delta. I was to take it over from former hunter Doug when his health started to wane. He spent most of his time in his tent compiling his memoirs but, I suspect, mostly thinking back on his good old hunting days. He reminded me in ways of the character in Hemingway's short story "The Snows of Kilimanjaro". In it, the hunter Harry lies dying in his tent in view of that magnificent mountain, the gangrene slowly eating his leg, having inflamed his darker side, not unlike our Doug.

Well before we rescued Bell, Doug had told us one evening around the fire that, if he was to come back, he'd like it to be as a male tree squirrel. "They spend most of their days lying in the sun and screwing. Then they get eaten." He was right about that: squirrels are much more sexually active than even rabbits. It's just their small litters that keep the population in check. Along with snakes, monkeys and hawks. You'll know when the males are heating up for the challenge, they make an urgent sound like someone turning a reluctant motor over and over. Belhauser was the only living thing I ever saw Doug show anything approaching affection. To this day I still have no idea how he came up with our squirrel's name.

But mine was a she, and boy was she cute. She loved to lick the ice in our drinks. Somewhat less endearing was that she also liked to chew through the insulation around electrical cables, as well as the flesh around my toes in bed. When we had clients in camp she would take to them as quickly as they to her. Belhauser was the honoured guest at every meal and had the run of the table. No one ever voiced an objection.

Another party trick was that she loved to hitch a ride on anyone's shoulder, or in a pocket. She would race up to the nearest person, scramble up their legs and then onto or into whichever perch she fancied. Guests fell for little Bell as hopelessly as we had, and they would fawn over the dear half wild creature. If she had not been seen around camp for some hours, invariably someone would ask after her.

The exception was one really dozy English guest who dismissed her as he did just about everything else in the place. It was not so much that he was not interested, it was more like he was disinterested. It seemed that he was perpetually distracted by voices in his head, although he was always frightfully cheerful and polite to us.

What happened was like that scene in the movie *Over the Hedge* where Crazy Squirrel moves so fast through the laser beams time slows down for everyone else. You've probably encountered something like it on a sidewalk when you find yourself walking towards someone, and you notice they've realised it too. You both step one way – the same way. So, you both step the other way ... until you find yourself nose to nose with an equally embarrassed stranger.

I was chatting to the rest of his group on our way back from a game drive. Old Doze Ball had not accompanied us on the drive, and we saw him walking towards us down the stone path towards the lunch boma. Belhauser was trotting along ahead of us. She had no intention of greeting the man and was bouncing past, thinking her own little seed-pod thoughts, when the man lurched to one side. His big-booted foot came down on the fragile skull – CRUNCH!

It seemed like we could feel the seismic crunch travel along the ground and up into our bodies. Time stopped. He looked down, said something like "oh" and carried on, smiling at us. All the others of his party were horrified, mortified, petrified on the spot. They looked at me. I could not find words to respond. There were none.

FOR FAIRLY OBVIOUS REASONS, DOGS are the favoured bush camp companions. All African hunters worth their kudu liver have a hunting dog, sometimes a pack of dogs. In traditional places like Transkei and Zululand, you can still see hunters with their *Canis africanis* packs striding across the veld in search of game: usually a small antelope or scrub hare. You even see some who have relocated to townships, scouring whatever is left of the local veld with their hunting packs.

It was pretty much for this reason that wild dogs, or wolves by another name, were originally domesticated: not as companions, but for hunting and keeping guard around the campfire at night for things big and beastly that might be roaming around with intent.

In its early years, some of the Kruger National Park rangers were noted for their dog packs, given that hunting back then was part of the job. In fact, for the first decade of the park's existence, killing predators in order to protect the plains game was their perceived role: no one had as yet given them any clear idea of what their job might actually be.

Most famous of the early rangers was Harry Wolhuter who is remembered primarily for the story of his having dispatched a very angry male lion with his sheath knife (both it and the animal's skin are preserved in the little museum at Skukuza rest camp).[33]

In fact, the ranger was attacked by two big, hungry lions (it was later found their bellies were completely empty). One treed him, but the other was chased off and kept at bay by Wolhuter's dog Bull. The faithful hound was one of three "rough Boer dogs" which had accompanied that particular patrol; all of them good lion dogs, as he called them. The other two, a bitch named Fly and an unnamed terrier mongrel, had stayed with the black rangers and the donkey train while the head ranger rode up ahead.

Wolhuter tells that his dogs were mostly all good lion dogs, but few of them would think of taking on a wild bushpig boar. Bushpigs would often lay waste to the mealie fields of subsistence farmers in the park, before the policy became to evict indigenous people living there. They with their dogs, and Wolhuter with his, would go after the porcine marauders, the dogs all held tightly on leads in order to keep them focused on the trail. This was after the time a cornered boar cut down six of the ranger's dogs before he caught up and dispatched it.

His best "pig" dog he bought in a village and named it Staunch. The dog, though not excessive in stature, could pull any man off his

---

[33] See the title story in *The Game Ranger, the Knife, the Lion and the Sheep.*

feet once he'd got on a bushpig's spoor. It very soon established itself as boss of the pack of some 25 mongrels. The arrival of an unnamed bull terrier nearly proved Staunch's nemesis. From day one they tore into one another, literally.

Wolhuter believed they should be left to fight it out, but they did so with such frequency and ferocity that eventually the ranger was forced to dispatch the newcomer whose body and spirit was being slowly broken. Staunch's own end came like that of most lions in natural conditions: once his condition declined he was attacked and killed by others in the pack.

A part Irish terrier named Pat was a real scrapper and could always be found at the centre of a pack fight. After one vicious brawl it was thought Pat had been killed but, while his grave was being dug, "pugnacious Pat" stood up, shook himself, and then flew right at the nearest dog.

Fly was a mongrel that resembled a deerhound; Wolhuter had taken her from a captured Boer wagon train during the Anglo-Boer War. She was extremely smart and devised many devious plans to steal food from cooking pots. Sometime after the lion incident she was taken by a crocodile in the Nwanetsi River.

Wolf, a mastiff-great Dane cross that was bought from an engine driver in Nelspruit, turned out to be one of Wolhuter's best lion dogs. At one time young Wolf had a narrow escape from a not-so-big croc in the Sweni "spruit". Some years later, however, he jumped into the Olifants River on a notably hot day and was gone in a splash, not to be seen again.

Another was a small Airedale-cross bitch named Biddy. She could hold on to a lion spoor for 24 hours without a break, never faltering other than for a drink. But she had one bad habit: the rangers would know when the lion was near because Biddy would begin a kind of feverish whimpering. This often caused the cat to make a break and the chase would continue. Once a lion had been shot, however, she was let off her leash and would tear into the carcass until spent.

She was one of some two dozen dogs that succumbed to a mysterious canine disease that in one season also killed off hundreds of "native" dogs. The fever did not kill her, but it made her so feeble and deranged her owner had to dispatch her. This is only the second time he expresses any kind of emotion in his entire autobiography[34] (it was most likely trypanosomiasis, or nagana, contracted from tsetse flies). The other time being, when the future ranger was still a youth, he was called upon to bury an entire family that had succumbed to malaria in their beds.

While the name Harry Wolhuter sits on the top bough of the tree of game ranger legends, the dog seated opposite him is of course Jock. Unlike the dogs belonging to hunters, Jock was a hound of a different breed, as much as was his owner, Percy (later Sir) FitzPatrick.

The dog was a pure, or almost pure-bred Staffordshire bull terrier, although the runt of his mother Jess's litter. Unlike the dedicated hunters who needed rough and disposable dogs, the wagon-train drivers, who carried supplies between the emerging Highveld gold fields and the Portuguese colonial coast, had the luxury as well as the incentive for breeding pure stock: selling the offspring for a good price.

Jock, being an unappealing offering, went to the most junior of the wagoneers for a song. And that was the beginning of what is surely South Africa's favourite dog tale. FitzPatrick worked on the wagon trail for only a year before rinderpest wiped out his entire team of oxen, whereafter he set off for the Rand. There he rose to become one of the golden Rand Lords and was later knighted for his "services to the empire": basically steering South Africa's monumental gold haul towards the seat of the empire in London. (It has been figured that, until South Africa's yield began to decline in the late 20th century, the country had supplied around 90 per cent of all the gold ever mined in all of history.)

The tale of Jock's adventures with his owner is thrilling, one of high drama as much as mutual affection. As much between Jock and Fitzpatrick as that between the hound and the huge Zulu "voorloper" Jim Mokokel. But the ending is heart-breaking. With the wagon sold to pay debts, and Percy off to seek fortune elsewhere, Jock was left in the care of a friend Tom who owned a store in the Lowveld. Jock guarded the store as well as the nearby chicken run and coop like a

---

[34] Harry Wolhuter, *Memories of a Game Ranger*, The Wildlife Protection and Conservation Society, 1948.

Spartan. However, at night he could not account for every jackal or opportunistic village hound, so chickens were being taken.

One night Tom heard a commotion in the chicken house and, seeing a doglike shape in the full-moon light and assuming it was a raider, let off a shot. All went quiet. In the morning the man found one dog obviously killed in a maul, and the other with a small red splotch on its chest. Jock had done his duty to the end.

Not all bush dog stories end in a mauling or with a bullet, but they do all end. Take Django, for example, surely one of the few pets to live in or around the Okavango Delta and to succumb to something other than a leopard, snake or a crocodile.

Sitting around the Skull Bar at Oddball's Camp, where a large crocodile skull sits as the pub trophy, you might learn of all the hounds that have been taken along those shores. As someone at the Duck Inn in Maun noted: the puppy you give someone at Christmas usually ends up as a python's New Year's dinner. But as has been implied, not Django, who lived a full and relatively lengthy life.

How the feisty little terrier was named begins with the death of Marmalade, long-time companion of Salome (a friend of mine who had relocated to Maun to marry grizzled game guide Peter). To help her get over the trauma, friends organised a "movie and popcorn" night. The film was a spaghetti western titled *Django Shoots First*: among the worst films ever made, according to Peter. Maun in the 1980s was not first in the queue for rental movies, for which you also had to locate a DVD player and lug in a generator to run the whole contraption.

The dog had been offered to Salome as a replacement pet by a woman camp manager friend whose own bitch had recently had a litter of four. But there was a not-so-small problem: the dog owner did not know that, by circuitous arrangement, the puppy in question had already been promised to someone else.

And, if that was not trouble enough, in a town where disputes might be settled with traditional weapons, not only was that other person a puffed up dowager on holiday in Botswana from her "country seat" on the Kenyan coast, she was also the mother of Bernadette. Bernadette owned the Duck Inn and was the most feared woman – possibly person – of the Delta. How it all worked out is a very funny and engaging story in all its detail, as is the entire book of the dog's life.[35]

From the time he could trot at walking pace, Django proved both fierce and fearless and, like Django in the movie, he always shot first. The wiry little terrier accompanied the family on safaris, be it by vehicle, by canoe – including mokoro – and even walking safaris; like the one all the way from Mombo Island to Maun with living legend Willie Phillips. When baby Skye followed not long after the arrival of Django, they made a very tight foursome. On one venture they came among what must rank among the most bizarre sights ever: a huge crocodile drifting down the Okavango River with half a human torso clamped in its jaws. Ah Africa, always something new.

In the end it was not a croc, a leopard, or even an eagle that took the little mop of bristly fur, but nothing bigger than a fly. *Glossina* sp. to be more specific. The family had been on safari with friends and driven through a cloud of tsetse flies, thinking not much of it since no one seemed to have been stung. However, some months later Django started acting most odd, walking round in circles and struggling to keep his balance. By the time it was diagnosed it was too late to treat.

Django had contracted nagana, trypanosomiasis, or tryps as vets say. When contracted by humans it's called sleeping sickness. You cannot say it's better to die from the bite of a fly, a crocodile taking you or a bullet through the heart, because the death of a loved one is always heart-breaking.

CONSERVATIONISTS CLIVE AND CONITA WALKER can lay claim to having among the most unusual and delightful camp (and house) guests ever. This story starts back in 1981 when they were party to the purchase of a modest game farm in the Waterberg that was to form the core of a private rhino reserve. Today, the resultant Lapalala Wilderness is a 48 000-hectare tract of wild bush stretching across a large chunk of Limpopo Province.

Together this highly effective couple (each with their own

---

[35] Peter Comley, *Django: The Small Dog with a Big Heart*, Jonathan Ball Publishers, 2013.

fascinating stories to tell, which they have done in various books), started not only the reserve, but also the Endangered Wildlife Trust, the Waterberg Biosphere Reserve and the Lapalala Wilderness School. To date the bush school has welcomed more than 80 000 learners and their teachers, as well as university students. While Clive was out and about doing game rangery-like things, Conita was busy with chores such as running a bush camp and raising bush orphans.

Among the many creatures rescued and mothered by Conita was a female hippo that was raised in their washroom. It was later released back into the Palala River where in time it produced its own offspring. Then there was the more traumatic experience of caring for a severely injured white rhino calf they named Moeng. But it is the story of Bwana that captured most people's hearts.

This little black rhino was born prematurely, abandoned by its mother and found wandering around the bush bleating morosely, with death its most likely fate. The Walkers brought it back to their garden, where it became a virtual family member and wildlife celebrity. One thing you could say about Bwana is, given how prehistoric and menacing an adult looks, it's ridiculous how gorgeous, almost cuddly, a baby rhino can be.

Also, how much a small mammal – just about every kind of mammal from mice to dolphins – needs a mother's love and care in order to reach maturity. Conita had to be that mother and Bwana would walk behind her, following at her heels, in order to maintain the feeling of safety it would have had from its own mother in the bush if things there had worked out differently.

In her book about Bwana,[36] Conita writes that the war on rhinos is as much about the targeted animals as it is about people. The plight of conservation is really about including poor rural people into the conservation conversation and raising human consciousness about what it really means to be human: which is, to treat all living things as sentient and venerated.

OF ALL CLINT EASTWOOD MOVIES the best least-known one is, in my opinion, *White Hunter, Black Heart*. It relates the story of film

---

[36] Conita Walker, *A Rhino in my Garden,* Jacana Media, 2017.

director John Huston (father of Angelica, played by Eastwood) who uses the filming of *The African Queen* as the means to attain his real goal: to shoot a big African tusker.

The scene where a massive African bull elephant tears out the tree line and bears down on the hunter (killing his gun bearer) is truly frightening for the viewer and leaves you wondering: how the hell did they film that!? The answer in just three letters is Abu. Remember that heartrending TV ad for some computer where an adult elephant helps a youngster up a sand bank? Abu.

Abu's handler in those days was the maverick, cigar-chomping American Randall Jay Moore. The man had pulled his first pay cheque shovelling mounds of elephant dung at a circus-aligned animal training facility in America. Randall liked Abu so much he endeavoured to build the mighty pachyderm its own safari lodge, but that was still all in the future. The back-story of Abu Camp in the Okavango Delta begins some two decades earlier...

By the most unlikely double accident, one day Moore found himself in Oregon as the owner of three elephants: his mentors at the training facility had been killed in two separate incidents, one following close on the other (the woman gored to death by an elephant in musth in front of a large circus audience in Canada, and the man stomped to death by his favourite pachyderm at base camp).

No one else in Oregon was going to adopt the huge animals that had been branded "killers" by the media. Randall, having worked with them, knew them to be otherwise, but what the heck was a young man of limited means going to do with these moving mountains? Turns out Randall proved to be as adept at PR as he was at caring for elephants. He hatched the plan to re-introduce them to their natural habitat, with backing from an American television network that would film his *Back to Africa* saga.

The Kenyan-based wildlife photographer, conservation oddity and New York fashionista Peter Beard had suggested that elephant-back safaris would be the ultimate African experience, so it was to East Africa they headed. The sea voyage was gruelling for humans and animals alike, with one handler dying from appendicitis, one elephant (Owalla) suffering severe seasickness, and another (Thsombe), dying from food poisoning soon after docking at Port Elizabeth.

But there things got snagged by the African red-tape worm. Once it was revealed the animals had been born in South Africa, they could not secure the necessary paperwork from the Kenyan side. At the time Pilanesberg Game Reserve was newly established and looking for animals to restock it. And so it was the two remaining animals, Orwalla and Durga, headed towards Sun City and their new and final home. Moore spent a full year with them there, overseeing their rewilding in the Pilanesberg, and he must have thought that would be that.

But 16 years later he received an urgent call from the park's veterinary staff: Owalla had been severely gored in a tussle with a hippo at a waterhole and had a gaping hole in one of her front legs. Attempts to dart her had failed and it was feared she would die if the wound could not be treated on the ground. And what then of the calf she had given birth to recently?

The American duly flew out and you might recall seeing the event that followed in our still-fresh television service in the early 1980s: a 4x4 approaches the female and her offspring and stops a safe way off. Randall Moore jumps out and walks up to the elephants, saying "trunk up, Orwalla, trunk up" and gesturing as he used to. Up goes her trunk and over walks Moore to greet his old friend. For the following few weeks he packed her wound with a poultice until she was well enough to heal on her own.

Having established himself as the world's foremost elephant whisperer, when the opportunity arose to make a movie of Dalene Matthee's story *Circles in the Forest* – one of the lead characters of which is a fearsome bull elephant – again a call went out to Randall Moore to help find such a beast. Not an actual wild one, mind, but a nice, already tame big tusker.

He phoned around and at a wildlife park in Grand Prairie, Texas, came upon a big bull named Abu. Not only was this old African immigrant a most placid beast among giants, he carried just the kind of substantial dentures the movie called for. At the time Abu was being kept in squalid conditions, but Moore immediately recognised that he had lucked upon an exceptional animal.

The trainer got his new protégé scrubbed up for the journey back to Africa. While at sea Moore taught Abu the basics of what would be asked of him, and the big bull easily picked a wide range of moves. In the actual film, during one climactic scene the animal known as "Old Foot" saves the lead (human) character from drowning by lifting him out of a stream with his tusks and gently laying him on the bank.

His faultless role in this as well as later films gained for the elephant its Hollywood stage name of "One-take Abu". But once again Randall Moore, having become the elephant's de facto manager, had to find a permanent home for his rising star. That's when he remembered Peter Beard's vision of riding elephants through the bush.

By this time Botswana had supplanted Kenya as the favoured safari destination, and in Microsoft gazillionaire, the late Peter Allen, he found a backer. Allan held a safari concession on the western edge of the Okavango Delta – what could be better? With Randall and lodge manager Michael Lorenz, the plan was to create the most unique safari destination in Africa, and so they did.

In order to build their own rideable herd, more elephants were sought, mostly rescue elephants from game culls in various game reserves, but also from inhumane imprisonment at safari parks. Abu Camp quickly earned its stars, as you might imagine (also its nut-squeezing prices). In the early days guests got to ride the elephants. However, with growing awareness of appropriate and inappropriate human–animal relations, this was supplanted by a "walking with elephants" encounter, and then to just enjoying their company in their overnight boma.

These days no direct contact is permitted between the Abu herd and lodge visitors, but they do get to see the line of grey bush galleons as they move out from the camp in the mornings to browse along the tree line out of camp, as well as on their return in the evening. The herd still sleeps in a safe, confined boma, but the plan is to ultimately rewild them completely.

But it has not been all fun in the African sun there. Abu was involved in a confrontation with a wild bull in which he sustained a severe leg injury. All the ministrations could not save him and in 2002 the remarkable animal succumbed to a heart attack. A male calf born to then camp herd matriarch Shireni in 2008 was named Baby Abu.

One thing about rearing and housing ostensibly wild animals is that, no matter how good-natured they might seem, they remain unpredictable. Returning from a marketing trip to New York one year, a trainer, or mahout, was busy working around his assigned animal. The female elephant was untethered and as its minder turned his back on her, she knocked him down and crushed him with her huge forehead. She had to be dispatched, as is the drill with all ostensibly wild animals that attack humans.

Death comes to us all, eventually. But how would you plan your end if indeed you could: with a bang from the head of an African elephant while you were still vital, or a whimper in some lonely room somewhere, frail and confused?

The Hunters, the Hunted and the Balance of Nature

IT'S EARTH DAY TODAY AND as I sit down to write the finale chapter to this book and I'm wondering what I'm going to say to Mother Nature about why we set fire to her planet. I imagine a conversation between her and us might go something like this:

Children, I turn my back for a moment and look at the mess you've made of things. What have you done with my chameleons, and my honeybees?

Ummm ...

And where are all my wild dogs, and my cheetahs?

Errr ...

(She looks under the sea) Where are the fish? And the sharks? You've even gone and lost all the crayfish and perlemoen for heaven's sake! What is wrong with you?! I give you gifts like rivers and flowers and birds and other animals and just look what you do? You go and make atom bombs and chain saws and drift nets. Just wait till your father gets home.

(Father gets home) You just don't listen to your mother, do you? I don't like to have to do this every time I come home but here we go....

Zap – Smallpox.

Owww!

Shazam – Spanish Flu.

Ouch!

Sim Sala Bim – Aids.

Whimper!

Fus Ro Dah – Covid!

Arrrgh!
And where are all my rhinos?

The census tell us that, over the past several decades, the populations of just about every large wild animal species in Africa, along with many of the smaller ones, have crashed alarmingly.[37] The numbers for even species such as zebra, wildebeest, buffalo and giraffe, also lions, at which we were not really looking because they seemed so ubiquitous and abundant, have started to nosedive.

While poaching is partly to blame is some cases, the overall cause is what the textbooks call the increasing human footprint, otherwise known as the population explosion. And while the rest of the world's population graphs have tapered off, or have started to, Africa's population continues to climb. More and more people, bigger and bigger towns, cities and sprawling townships, and less and less nature. More and more marginal farmlands being hacked into the bush, more people scrounging off the land any way they can. More and more bush meat being taken, animal parts being "harvested" for vanity trinkets and quackery potions.

When I was born, falling wildlife numbers were not yet news. By the time my children were born we were down to around 50 per cent of the numbers that had remained more or less constant since the Ark grounded. My granddaughter, just starting school, might but might not live to see much of our wildlife in the actual wilds.

Poor communities have mushroomed around the game parks: environmental devastation on one side of the fence and abundance on the other. How do we expect that to play out? Not nearly enough has been done to uplift the rural poor, let alone the urban ones, so we can expect poaching to escalate (bearing in mind that the poachers are often the foot soldiers of international crime cartels). The current poaching inside the Kruger Park is the tip of our own wedge of

---

[37] According to the IUCN Red Data List the black rhino population is down around 96% from historical numbers; the southern white rhino population has bounced from an estimated historical number of one million or more, to just 20 or fewer 100 years ago, to around 18 000 today; but the northern white rhino is officially extinct in the wild; forest elephants are down 86% and savanna elephants 60% over the past 50 years; cheetah more than 90%; and the African wild dog an estimated 95%, maybe more.

economic disparity. Even in zoos targeted animals are no longer safe.[38]

And yet the reality is that we are nothing in the bigger scheme, whatever that might be. Our time on Earth will be as a brief candle and so far we have been pretty poor players on our stage. It is estimated that 99.9 per cent of all species that ever lived have gone extinct.[39] And that about a million of those living today will go extinct this century. What can we deduce from this data? That whoever is in charge of this thing is extremely wasteful (waste-full) or careless (care-less). Pick a number and get in line, it looks like you might be up next *Homo sapiens*.

Possibly the most flabbergasting thing about the story of life on Earth is that at every one of the billions of division points along the evolutionary road from algae to human, the survival coin was flipped and what we see today is simply a result of which side the coin fell: heads you move onwards and upwards, tails and it's ta-ta. If you won, you were given a ticket for the next coin flip. By turns it was tails and game over for Hallucigenia and Wiwaxia in the wake of the Cambrian Explosion around 500 mya, cheerio the lobe-finned fish 100 million years later, so long T-rex, au revoir sabre-tooth cats, adios Neanderthals, arrivederci Dodo, totsiens bluebuck, hamba kahle quagga and hope to see you later rhinos.

I CONFESS I GREW UP shooting at things like birds and rabbits with my BSA pellet gun (although not very successfully you will be relieved to learn), but I later set to watching them instead. At some point I found myself in an anti-aircraft outfit having to learn how to distinguish a Mirage from a Mig (I was not very good at that either).

It was called getting the "giss", apparently an acronym from the Second World War aircraft reconnaissance: you were trained to recognise the "general impression, size and shape" of a plane at a glance, to distinguish friend from foe, and so know whether or not to blast it out of the sky. Birders learn to do much the same and they use the same word for it.

---

[38] See: "Rhino shot dead by poachers at French zoo", *The Guardian*, 7 March 2017.
[39] See: www.pbs.org/wgbh/evolution/extinction/massext/statement.

If you've spent time photographing birds, you'll know that, all too often, as soon as you focus attention on the subject it lets off a white stream, leans forward and flies off. It's as though they were Shrödinger's birds: as soon as you observe them you alter the perceived reality of the situation. The bird is either perched or flying, depending on whether or not you look at it.

The longer you observe something the more you notice about it. Not just general things like size and shape, but also flight pattern, colour, habitat and behaviour. What makes a robin-chat different from a chat, a whimbrel from a curlew, or a lark from a pipit? For a hunter these things mean life or death, for you or your prey. It teaches you to be quiet, both within and without, something we find so hard to do in our busy modern lives.

I was recently reminded by an old colleague of mine, who shall remain nameless, about the time we went on a walking trail, together with some other more urban types, in the northern Kruger National Park. We had been well briefed on how to respond in the event of possible encounters, to be vigilant and to walk in silence until instructed to stop and discuss something. After a short while I could tell our guide was getting agitated with all the chatter, as was I.

I managed to keep it in until, on the third day, after we had just managed to evade a herd of buffaloes and the yakking reached monkey-in-trouble level. I asked said colleague to give me his notebook and pencil (we were journalists and used to carry these things). I would not have remembered but recently he showed me the piece of paper on which I'd written:

A Meditation on Reasons Not to Talk When Walking in the Bush

Human speech, more than any other noise, alerts and disturbs wild animals. The more you talk the less you see.

The rangers need to have their senses clear to read the bush and be aware of possible danger. Chatting interferes with this.

Chatter brings attention to "things" but blocks your ability to "walk like a hunter" – to assimilate the signs and sense of the bush.

Talking brings with it the rush and clatter of urban life. Wilderness is about silence.

It irritates other trailists.

I must have been really peeved to be so pedantic at the time. They all probably thought I was a bird watcher.

THIS CALLED TO MIND A scene in the film *The Great Dance: A Hunter's Story* (made by the Foster brothers, one of whom, Craig, went on to make *My Octopus Teacher*) where a Bushman hunter tells someone where the leopard whose spoor they are attempting to track has gone. What he answered was something akin to: "It went over that dune, then it stopped in the shade of a guarri bush, then it took a small steenbok and pulled it up into a camelthorn."

How did he know all that? It was what he did when he walked as a hunter, he said: he became the leopard. Some call it walking like a hunter. Some wise people have observed that not just humans, but all living creatures, have souls, that everything in nature is spiritual and is in fact God materialised (he made it all, after all). As much as this is evident in the close study of San rock art, that everything is connected on a spiritual plane, so too is it for the American First People for whom Bear was a brother and even Rattlesnake was grandfather.

In the Bleek-Lloyd manuscript[40] housed in the Jagger Library at Cape Town University (and all praise to the spirits, it was not destroyed in the great fire of 2021 that razed the building), a shaman revealed to the German anthropologist Wilhelm Bleek that when he went "underwater", into a hallucinogenic trance, there were many dangers one had to confront in order to reach the supreme spirit !Kaggan. Massive spirit serpents and mean-mouthed predators abounded.

Hunters, in the traditional meaning, are bound up in a sacred relationship not only with the animal they are hunting but also with all animals, and in fact with everything in the great circle of things. The hunter is just one small part of the totality of nature. If he is not (invariably it is a "he"), he will have no success as a hunter and he and his people will go hungry. Along with that relationship comes responsibility and respect, to animal, nature, family – all depend on one another for their individual survival.

The way of the hunter is also the way of the lover. It is a state

---

[40] See *Stories of the Veld III, Of Hominins, Hunter-Gatherers and Heroes: 20 Amazing Places in South Africa,* chapter 10, "Kamberg, Game Pass Shelter".

of grace beyond the rational. Everything exists only as it is part of everything else. You are who you are by the twin legacy of how you reside in others and how you move through your own environment. We can think of it as a kind of organic Ubuntu.

The old way was to live with and among the wild animals: how else, when humans were few and the wild things were many? There is an old Bushman tradition that when a new lion moves into a territory, things need to be discussed. A group of hunters will sneak up on it while it is sleeping and lay into it with knobkerries. Once the confused animal has gathered its wits, it will appreciate there are the limits to its power.

But this all changed when our ancestors began to tame animals. Suddenly a cow in a kraal, or a pig in a sty, was no spiritual being but rather, and very simply, food. Even worse was that the domestication of animals turned us, their human minders and consumers, into slave owners. We became careless killers of the same animals that were once not only our kin, not only those we feared, but also our animal spirits, our totems and our spirit gods.

It's most likely that fear was the factor leading to the domestication of wild dogs, jackals and wolves by any name. It's also pretty certain that it happened wherever there were people huddled in the dark, in a cave, or around a fire, surrounded by darkness. A dog-ancestor hanging around a camp once the humans had retired made for a very good security alarm. A pack of dogs was even better.

You can imagine that scraps might be left around the fire to entice the canines. Once they were comfortable around humans they made for excellent trackers or sled pullers (the domestication of canines is believed to have occurred in several distinct places, one being among the Sami as sled dogs). It was fear, later work, far more than any notion of companionship that gifted us our best friends.

It is believed the first humans arrived in North America somewhat more than 20 000 years ago. It took them just a few thousand years to hunt to extinction the woolly mammoths, a giant armadillo, three species of camel, a giant ground sloth, a giant bison, four species of antelope and several species of horses among about 30 kinds of large animals (the modern horses, so emblematic of the West, arrived with

Spanish conquistadors about 600 years ago).

The story of Australia is much the same. When humans first arrived there, a place where the animals would not have known how to deal with two-legged predators, it signalled the end of the evolutionary road for the marsupial lion, along with one in four large animals and another 10 smaller ones.

What if the idea of indigenous people taking only that which they needed for immediate survival might turn out to be only a matter of opportunity? Remember what Archimedes said about having a lever long enough and a fulcrum strong enough to hold it and he could lift the Earth?

Once we got our levers and our fulcrums we took atoms, split them and made bombs to blow people to smithereens; we made nets big enough to clean out the oceans and chainsaws to clear-cut the forests. As that great spirit Mohandas K. Gandhi said, the Earth has enough for everyone, but it does not have enough for everyone's greed.

For the past four of five decades I have felt like a bystander at some environmental smack-down, wondering what all these crazy fools think they're up to! Being a greenie is to be burdened with the Curse of Cassandra. She was the daughter of King Priam of Troy and, when she tried to warn him about the dangers of the approaching wooden horse, she was thrown to the Greeks (the different versions of the story offer varied narratives, but none of them ends well for her).

It's does no good to be able to foresee the future, as environmentalists have been doing at least since I got wind of the climate change scenario at university. We were given the data and it was not good: pollution numbers were sky-rocketing along with human populations, while wildlife and natural habitat figures were teetering on a slippery slope.

But I've started to change my mind about all that. I think we've started to appreciate, on some collective level, just what we have thrown away. It started for me when I read *The Greenpeace Chronicles* by Greenpeace founder member Robert Hunter. Here were people prepared to make waves big time,[41] throwing small speedboats as well

---

[41] They first identified themselves as the Don't Make A Wave anti-nuclear arms testing organisation.

as their bodies against warships and whaling fleets.

At first much of the rest of the world regarded them as renegades, hippies and even communist-sponsored terrorists, but I felt these were my kinds of people. (Funny thing there is that the first anti-whaling actions were taken against Soviet whaling factory fleets.)

Today in many parts of the world, Greenpeace, along with various green groups and political parties, have entered the mainstream. Some people still regard them as crazies, but we can thank them for the fact that we still have any whales left at all. We can thank David Attenborough for giving us a magnificent view of what pristine nature looks like, how it used to look, and how it could look again. And we can thank Greta Thunberg and her army of young environmental crusaders for, maybe, saving the entire planet as we know it.

My peers and I grew up singing and memorising the words of all the Bob Dylan songs and we believed that the times they were a-changing, that we'd stand over the graves of all the masters of war and that a hard rain was a-gonna fall. Those formative times influenced my view of things and betimes I have marched to end apartheid and to free Mandela, against nuclear power, pollution and, more recently, against state capture.

But I keep on coming back to the one song "I Threw It All Away" from Nashville Skyline (one of his better if lesser-known albums). It tells – warns, I suppose – of that all-too-common human failing of not realising all the good things we have until we throw them away.

And so when we sit under a marula or a thorn tree somewhere, with our sundowner drinks, watching herds of antelope sweeping majestically across the plains, we should remember to salute the game rangers, the wildlife researchers, the Black Mambas of the South African Lowveld, the Akashinga warriors of the Zambezi Valley and everyone who has put their life on the line out there in the tangled African bush.

The alternative scenario, my friend, is blowing in the wind.

Other books by David Bristow.

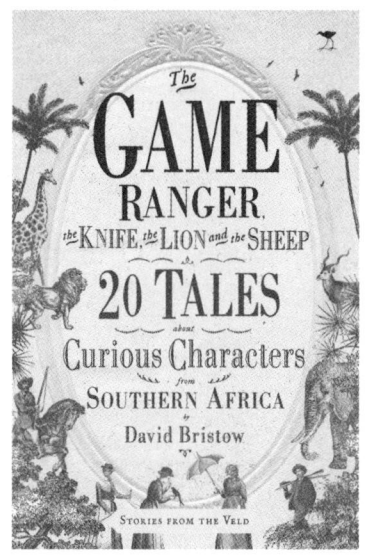